Parents Guide: Navigating Through Autism with Hope

Kenneth Perry

Parents Guide: Navigating Through Autism with Hope

©2023

ISBN: 9798856893976

TABLE OF CONTENTS

Foreword

When my daughter Adriana was diagnosed with autism at the age of three, my wife and I felt like we had been plunged into a vast ocean with no land in sight. We loved our little girl deeply, but we didn't know the first thing about autism or how to help her. Like many parents in our situation, we struggled to come to terms with the diagnosis and had no idea where to turn for guidance.

The months following Adriana's diagnosis were filled with confusion, anxiety, and constant searches for information. We devoured book after book, scoured websites, joined online parenting groups, attended online seminars given by so-called experts. But instead of becoming clearer, the path forward only seemed more obscured. We received contradictory advice, alarming statistics, and definitive proclamations that only further undermined our confidence.

Desperate for answers, we allowed ourselves to be bombarded by theories, treatments, and purported cures. We spent thousands of dollars on special diets, supplements, therapies, you name it. Well-meaning friends and family added to the noise, sharing anecdotes and articles, convinced they had discovered some vital truth we were missing.

But nothing seemed to help, and the clamor of voices only grew louder. We started to feel overwhelmed and hopeless. The promise of quick fixes gave way to the reality that there were no easy answers. Our beautiful, sensitive, fascinating daughter was her own unique person. We needed to put aside the expert opinions and external noise, and focus on truly understanding her.

Slowly, we learned to find the signal through the noise. We discovered the power of observing her closely to discern what made her tick. We let her take the lead in play and exploration, following her interests rather than forcing our own agenda. We surrounded her with loving support and worked patiently to expand her skills. Of course there were still moments of doubt and frustration, but we developed confidence in our ability to give her what she needed most: unwavering love and acceptance.

Our faith in God was crucial in moving forward during this difficult period. Through prayer and relying on God's plan for Adriana, we found the strength and hope to take each day as it came.

Along the way, we gained the wisdom to tune out voices that breed fear, anger, and misinformation. We became active partners in Adriana's care, trusting our instincts and making informed choices after careful consideration. We sought evidence-based therapies that were tailored to her specific needs. We shifted our focus from changing who she was to bolstering her strengths. Above all, we never lost sight of the remarkable, sensitive, funny girl we knew and loved.

In writing this book, my greatest hope is to empower other parents who are embarking on this journey with their child. But autism cannot be summarized in a simple guide. Each child's needs are unique, and only you can be the expert on your own son or daughter. My advice is to trust God and put one foot in front of the other each day, keep learning additional knowledge and experience, and drown out the cacophony of misguided voices. With patience, compassion and resilience, you will gain clarity amid the chaos.

Though the way will not always be smooth, you can move forward with love, hope and celebration of the wonderful child you have been gifted. My darling Adriana continues to blossom every day. Her diagnosis has come to feel less like a tragedy and more like a remarkable twist in her story, revealing untold depths beneath a beautiful surface. Our family has been tested during this period, but we know in the end we will be endlessly enriched by walking this path with her.

Wherever you stand today in your own journey with autism, please know you do not walk alone. Trust God and he will direct your paths for yourself and your child. Let it be your compass, guiding you through stormy seas toward the clarity and peace that lie ahead. With God's love and nurturing, you will find your way.

Chapter 1

Introduction to Autism Spectrum Disorder

Autism Spectrum Disorder (ASD) refers to a range of complex neurological and developmental conditions characterized by challenges with social skills, communication, and restricted or repetitive behaviors. Autism exists on a spectrum because there is wide variation in the type and severity of symptoms each person experiences. According to the Centers for Disease Control, around 1 in 44 children are diagnosed with ASD today.

ASD begins early in childhood and causes delays or impairments in many areas of development. While autism is usually diagnosed in early childhood, some milder cases may not be recognized until later ages. With appropriate support, treatment, and accommodations, people with autism can lead very fulfilling lives. This guide will provide parents with essential information and strategies to help understand their child, advocate for their needs, and improve their development and wellbeing.

Common Characteristics and Behaviors

No two people with autism are exactly alike, but they share certain tendencies that are important to recognize. Some of the most common characteristics associated with ASD include:

- Difficulties with social communication and interaction - This can include challenges making eye contact, reading social cues, making conversation, and developing age-appropriate friendships. Children may seem disinterested in others, appear detached or avoidant in social situations. They may have trouble understanding the give-and-take of conversations, struggle to interpret facial expressions and body language, or not pick up on subtle cues that regulate social interactions. Difficulty empathizing with others and understanding different perspectives is also common.

- Repetitive or restricted behaviors and interests - Unusual mannerisms like rocking, flapping, or spinning are common. Often children develop intense, special interests in specific topics or objects that border on obsession. They may amass vast amounts of knowledge about highly specific subjects, play repetitively with certain toys, or rigidly insist on adhering to peculiar routines. Deriving comfort from sameness and deep aversion to changes in routine are hallmark traits.

- Sensory issues - Heightened or reduced sensitivity to stimuli like sound, light, texture, smell or taste. Responses like covering ears to noise, fascination with lights, avoiding certain textures, sniffing objects, or extreme picky eating are common in autism. Some crave sensory input and seek activities like spinning, jumping, singing loudly or rubbing surfaces. Others find sensory stimuli easily overwhelming and withdraw or have meltdowns when overstimulated.

- Speech and language deficits - Delayed or absent speech is a core symptom. Impaired conversational ability, odd or repetitive speech, literal interpretation of figurative phrases, and difficulty understanding nuances in language are also seen. Those who develop language often have deficiencies in areas like vocabulary, grammar, pitch, volume, rhythm, and social appropriateness of what they say.

- Cognitive and learning challenges - Around 50% of those with autism have average to above-average intelligence. But all struggle in areas like focusing, comprehension, following multi-step instructions, processing information, problem-solving and organization. Learning disabilities are common, including challenges with reading, writing and math. Abstract thinking, imagination and concept formation tend to be areas of weakness.

- Motor skill impairments - Physical clumsiness, an odd gait or posture, poor coordination and abnormal body movements like hand flapping or toe walking are often present. Activities requiring fine motor skills like writing or using utensils can be frustrating. Gross motor delays may cause late walking or struggles with running, jumping or climbing.

- Behavioral challenges - Difficulty regulating emotions can cause frequent outbursts, aggression, or self-injury. Distress often results from disruption in routine, inability to communicate needs, or overstimulation. Some exhibit intense tantrums, laughing or crying spells for no apparent reason, or lack of impulse control. Self-soothing behaviors like rocking or spinning are common when stressed.

- Sleep disturbances - Insomnia, frequent night waking and early rising often disrupt sleep. Melatonin deficiency, anxiety, sensory issues and gastrointestinal discomfort can interfere with quality sleep. Establishing proper sleep hygiene is important but challenging.

- Feeding problems - Picky eating, food aversions, cravings for certain textures and obsessive mealtime routines are frequently seen. Some have oral motor deficits making chewing or swallowing difficult. Many are highly sensitive to food textures and temperatures. Nutritional deficits are common.

- Anxiety and depression - Many with ASD develop comorbid conditions like anxiety, OCD or mood disorders. Sensory overload, social difficulties and coping with change often manifest as excessive worrying. Clinical depression may result from isolation and communication struggles.

- Intellectual disability - Around 31% of those with ASD have some degree of intellectual impairment, while 24% have an IQ in the normal range. Those deemed "high-functioning" have average or high intelligence but still struggle with social communication, behavior and cognition.

Autism occurs in all racial, ethnic and socioeconomic groups but is 4-5 times more common in boys than girls. Some co-occurring disorders like ADHD, gastrointestinal issues, epilepsy and sleep disorders are also more prevalent. Though autism itself does not directly impact life expectancy, higher mortality rates are seen due to factors like accidental injury and seizures.

Causes and Risk Factors

The exact causes of ASD are not fully understood, but research suggests autism likely results from a combination of genetic and environmental factors influencing early brain development.

- Genetics - Autism tends to run in families, indicating a strong genetic component. Those with a sibling or parent with autism are at substantially higher risk. Specific gene mutations and chromosomal abnormalities like Fragile X syndrome have been linked to autism.

- Brain structure - Structural differences in areas controlling social functioning, communication, reasoning and behavior regulation are often seen. Imbalances in brain chemicals like serotonin, oxytocin and GABA may also play a role.

- Prenatal environment - Advanced parental age, maternal illness during pregnancy, extreme prematurity, and exposure to heavy metals or toxins may increase autism risk. High levels of prenatal testosterone is a hypothesized risk factor.

- Complications of labor and delivery - Oxygen deprivation, umbilical cord complications, low birth weight, and jaundice have been linked to heightened risk for autism.

- Immune system abnormalities - Autoimmune reactions, chronic neuroinflammation, and maternal antibodies attacking fetal brain tissue may be implicated. But more research is needed.

- Gastrointestinal issues - Digestive problems and abnormal gut bacteria observed in many with autism has led some to hypothesize it stems from immune reactions to foods or imbalanced gut microbiome.

- Environment issues – Problems may be caused by exposure to toxins in the environment including mold, chemicals, and other substances that can result in adverse reactions during early development of a child.

Despite substantial research, no definitive cause for autism has emerged. In most cases it likely arises from a matrix of genetic vulnerabilities interacting with environmental triggers during crucial developmental windows. There is a lot of discussion about how vaccines might be included in this group. We will not cover this in the book, but parents should research this topic further. Ongoing studies continue investigating theories and risk factors.

Early Signs and Symptoms

ASD symptoms emerge in early childhood, usually before age 3 but sometimes later. Early signs can be subtle, but prompt evaluation and treatment greatly benefits long-term prognosis. Following are some hallmark indicators of autism in infants and toddlers to monitor carefully:

- Not babbling, pointing, or using gestures by 12 months
- Not speaking any words by 18 months
- Regression or plateauing of language after acquiring some words
- Failure to respond to name being called by 12 months

- Poor eye contact and lack of warm, joyful facial expressions

- Lack of interest in other children or sharing enjoyment

- Delayed imaginative play or tendency to play with toys rigidly

- Over- or under-reaction to sensory input like loud noises or textures

- Excessive lining up of toys, obsessed with parts of objects

- Repetitive motions like rocking, spinning, flapping, or hand twisting

- Unusually high or low activity level and attention span

- Tantrums, aggression, or head banging if routines disrupted

- Not pointing at objects to direct others' attention

- Appears in own world, tuned out or difficult to engage

If any loss of speech, social interest or other developmental milestones occurs, prompt evaluation for autism is crucial. Early indicators in infants are inability to make eye contact, lack of back-and-forth gestures or facial expressions, and not responding to name after one year of age. By age two, absence of meaningful two-word phrases or engaging in imaginative play are red flags. Failure to speak by 18-24 months warrants immediate assessment.

Since autism is neurological rather than psychological, children do not outgrow symptoms without intervention. But intensive early treatment during ages 2-3 has the best chance of improving outcomes. Parents should trust instincts and pursue evaluations even if pediatricians downplay concerns. Early diagnosis sets the stage for vital behavioral, educational and family therapies to help the child reach their full potential.

The Diagnostic Process

The process of diagnosing autism is multifaceted, involving developmental history, detailed observations, psychological testing, and input from parents and teachers. These combine to identify deficits in social communication and restrictive, repetitive patterns of behavior—the core domains of autism spectrum disorder.

No single medical test can diagnose autism. But the following assessments help identify or rule out other potential causes for concerning symptoms:

- Genetic testing - Chromosomal microarrays and testing for Fragile X, MECP2 duplication syndrome and other autism-related genetic abnormalities.
- Neurological exam - Assesses brain structure, nerve health, balance, coordination and involuntary movements that may indicate seizure disorders or other neurological conditions.
- Hearing and vision tests - Since sensory issues are common in ASD, it is important to ensure a child's hearing and vision are intact and not hindering development.
- EEG - Measures electrical activity in the brain to detect potential seizure disorders co-occurring with autism.
- Sleep studies - Given the prevalence of sleep disturbances, overnight polysomnograms help assess for issues like sleep apnea.

- Gastrointestinal evaluation - Since digestive issues often accompany autism, tests to rule out problems like reflux, food allergies, inflammation or malabsorption may be useful.

Ultimately, a comprehensive diagnostic evaluation of behavioral, social, motor, language, cognitive and adaptive skills is required based on criteria defined in the Diagnostic and Statistical Manual of Mental Disorders (DSM-5), the authoritative resource for psychiatric diagnoses.

To meet DSM-5 criteria for autism spectrum disorder, a child must exhibit persistent deficits in social communication and interaction, plus restricted patterns of behavior, interests or activities. Symptoms must be present from early childhood, cause significant impairment, and cannot be better explained by an intellectual disability.

Three levels specify severity based on how much support a person requires for everyday functioning:

- Level 1: Requiring support for deficits in social communication and restrictive behaviors.
- Level 2: Requiring substantial support due to impaired verbal and nonverbal communication skills, limited social engagement, and restrictive/repetitive behaviors appearing frequently enough to be obvious to casual observers.

- Level 3: Requiring very substantial support for severe deficits in communication skills and behavioral flexibility; difficulty coping with change causes great distress.

Meeting the full diagnostic criteria warrants a formal diagnosis of autism spectrum disorder. Milder variations like Asperger syndrome and pervasive developmental disorder-not otherwise specified (PDD-NOS) used in prior editions were folded into the umbrella autism spectrum disorder diagnosis in 2013.

Obtaining a thorough diagnostic evaluation from a specialist like a developmental pediatrician, psychiatrist, neuropsychologist or clinical psychologist experienced in assessing autism is essential before pursuing intervention services. Educational psychologists can also conduct evaluations required for school services eligibility. Diagnosis should not be rushed; it may require multiple appointments to complete the full assessment battery.

Throughout the process, parents serve a vital role providing detailed developmental history and advocating for their child's needs every step of the way. Asking questions, taking notes and tracking symptoms at home helps inform clinicians. If any aspects of testing or clinical impressions feel unsatisfactory, seeking a second opinion is perfectly valid. An accurate, well-substantiated diagnosis opens doors to support services and tailoring treatment to maximize outcomes.

Processing an Autism Diagnosis

Receiving confirmation that your child has autism understandably elicits myriad reactions. Parents often describe Shock, sadness, anger, despair, guilt, isolation, exhaustion—sometimes cycling rapidly through several emotions all at once. Feelings of mourning what you envisioned for your child's future are also normal. The road ahead seems daunting and unfamiliar. But amid the turbulence, one priority eclipses all—securing your child the best possible care and therapies at this pivotal window.

- Seek counseling - Processing painful emotions with a therapist nurtures resilience to weather challenges positively. Joining a support group connects you to other families facing similar hurdles.
- Educate yourself - Learn everything about ASD, available treatments and resources. Subscribe to autism blogs, journals and newsletters. Knowledge equips you to optimize care.
- Make self-care a priority - From proper rest and nutrition to stress management and maintaining relationships, caring for your own needs enables you to be fully present and energized for your child.
- Embrace your child - Rather than grieving for an imagined child, focus on accepting, connecting with and delighting in the actual child before you—unique talents, personality quirks, special interests and all.
- Trust your instincts - You know your child better than anyone. If something in their treatment or education feels off, speak up. Becoming their dedicated advocate optimizes their care.

- Be proactive - Once initial emotions settle, shift focus to actionable steps: securing treatment services, understanding legal protections, connecting with other families. Move forward purposefully.
- Find joy in small milestones - Each tiny step forward your child makes—new word uttered, gesture learned, food tried—is absolutely worth celebrating. Focus on progress.
- Hang on to hope - Though the road is long, with proper treatment and support many people with autism live happy, fulfilling and independent lives. Believe in your child's potential.

With time, information and support, most families adjust well and develop great capacity to nurture their child's growth. Patience, flexibility and fierce love for your child smooth the path ahead. Though emotionally taxing at times, the autism journey also offers profound rewards as you gain perspective on what matters most in life.

Treatment and Therapeutic Interventions

Though autism has no cure, many effective interventions and therapies help improve specific abilities and quality of life. Applied behavioral analysis (ABA), speech therapy, occupational therapy and medications are often incorporated into a comprehensive treatment plan tailored to the individual. Consistency, intensity and early intervention offer the best outcomes.

Educational interventions like ABA focus on improving social, behavioral, cognitive, motor and adaptive life skills. Speech-language therapy builds communication and social interaction abilities. Occupational therapy develops sensorimotor, adaptive and self-care skills. Medications help manage co-occurring conditions like anxiety, GI symptoms or hyperactivity. Additional treatments like sensory integration therapy address sensory processing issues.

- Applied Behavior Analysis (ABA) - The most extensively researched and commonly utilized autism intervention uses principles of learning and motivation to enhance socially appropriate behaviors and reduce problem ones. Key techniques include differential reinforcement, modeling, prompting and discrete trial teaching to motivate positive behaviors. ABA therapists work one-on-one with the child in a highly structured manner, continually assessing progress. ABA is considered most effective when initiated early, performed consistently for multiple years, and involves 35-40 hours per week of therapy. Many health insurance plans now cover ABA services.

- Early Intensive Behavioral Intervention (EIBI) - This is ABA therapy provided intensively soon after diagnosis, ideally by age 3. Delivered over multiple years, EIBI equips children with core skills like speech, social abilities, self-care and pre-academic concepts when brains are rapidly developing yet highly malleable. The substantial time commitment and costs of high-quality EIBI are challenging, but research confirms early intensive ABA greatly improves outcomes, reducing long-term educational and care expenses. Many parents become active therapists themselves, embedded in daily activities.

- Speech-language therapy - Practicing sounds, gestures, conversation skills, body language and prosody of speech reinforces communication abilities. Picture-based systems like PECS are commonly used to augment verbal skills. Social stories and video modeling help build conversation abilities and perspective-taking. PROMPT (Prompts for Restructuring Oral Muscular Phonetic Targets) is another specialized speech therapy using tactile cues to help shape mouth movements needed for clear speech. It focuses on physiologic components like jaw, lip, and tongue positioning to develop motor plans for intelligible speaking. Skills gradually transition from clinical to natural environments to promote generalization. Most children benefit from multiple weekly speech therapy sessions. Group therapy also provides social learning opportunities to practice communication skills with peers.

- Occupational therapy (OT) - Developing fine motor skills, sensorimotor integration, posture and optimal responses to sensory input are OT goals. Activities to strengthen hand-eye coordination, grasp, manipulation, writing or feeding skills are targeted. OT also helps with adapting tasks and environments to enable success and independence. Sensory gyms with special equipment provide sensory integration therapy.

- Physical therapy (PT) - For those with motor impairments, PT improves balance, coordination, core strength, and fine/gross motor abilities. Assistive equipment like orthotics may be utilized. Therapy often occurs in stimulating environments integrating sensory and social components. This facilitates generalizing movement skills to interactive situations.

- Music and art therapies - For some, music skills emerge before speech. Melodic intonation therapy uses singing to improve prosody and speech production. Music also provides sensory integration and calming effects. Creating visual art allows self-expression and developing motor coordination in engaging ways. Both build communication, social and regulation skills.

- Social skills groups - Led by specialists, these classes give students with autism the chance to learn and practice social interaction together. Role playing, video modeling, scripting and peer feedback build skills in areas like eye contact, reciprocity, reading cues, body language and perspective taking. Groups also provide friendship opportunities.

- Dietary and nutritional approaches - No evidence conclusively supports special diets, but some parents anecdotally report benefits from removing gluten, dairy and other potentially inflammatory foods. Due to picky eating, supplements may help fill nutritional gaps that can impact health and behavior. Getting lab testing done to check vitamin, mineral, and omega-3 levels can reveal specific deficiencies to target. For example, low ferritin, zinc, or vitamin D are common in ASD. Based on lab results, supplements of iron, magnesium, vitamin B6, vitamin D, or omega-3s may be warranted to restore optimal levels. Probiotics and digestive enzymes also help some with gastrointestinal issues. Other alternative remedies like melatonin are low-risk and may yield positive effects on sleep. Consulting a nutritionist knowledgeable about nutritional approaches for autism helps develop healthy, balanced eating habits to nourish the child's growth and healing.

- Medication - While medications don't treat autism's core symptoms, they are sometimes used to manage challenging behaviors or comorbid conditions like anxiety, inattention or obsessive tendencies that interfere with progress. However, the benefits of medications must be weighed carefully against risks. Drugs can mask underlying issues that would be better served through behavioral and natural approaches aimed at the root causes. Relying on meds alone runs the risk of stunting development by not addressing dysfunctional patterns and skill deficits appropriately. Antipsychotics, stimulants, antidepressants and anti-seizure meds are sometimes prescribed, but carry risks of significant side effects. Parents are encouraged to thoroughly educate themselves on any proposed medication, get multiple opinions, start low and go slow, and frequently reassess the need. Whenever possible, non-drug interventions to treat the child's specific challenges should be explored first, before considering pharmacological options. Medication may play a role, but should not replace holistic behavioral therapies.

Selecting treatments requires some trial and error, as each child responds differently. Maintaining detailed therapy notes, tracking data and communicating frequently with your team yields the greatest insights on which interventions are most impactful. While intensive early intervention is ideal, ABA and speech therapies prove beneficial well into the school-age and teenage years for developing social skills.

Chapter 2

Early Signs and Getting a Diagnosis

Recognizing the early red flags of autism and pursuing formal assessment is key to getting children the support they need as early as possible. While every child develops at their own pace, certain signs warrant discussion with your pediatrician and evaluation by specialists. This chapter covers developmental milestones to monitor, details of the diagnostic process, and coping emotionally with an autism diagnosis.

Evaluating Developmental Milestones

There are some behaviors that may indicate a risk for autism emerging in infants and toddlers. Bringing up any concerns with your child's doctor is recommended, even though early delays do not necessarily mean autism. Some signs to keep in mind include:

- By 6 months - Lack of back-and-forth babbling, smiling or other reactions to caregivers, focus on faces or voices. Limited grasping or reaching for objects within view. Typically developing 6 month olds engage in joint attention, exchanging smiles and sounds with caregivers. An absence of these beginning social engagement behaviors is an early red flag.

- By 9 months - No babbling, crawling, pointing or other gestures by 9 months. Little interest in interactive social games like patty cake, peekaboo or imitation. 9 months is when early pretend play like pretending to talk on a toy phone typically emerges. Lack of imitating gestures or seeking social games signals risk.

- By 12 months - No attempts to imitate speech or actions, use of single words like "dada" or "mama", or waving goodbye. Lack of response to own name being called. One year olds are usually exchanging simple words meaningfully and turning when their name is said. This foundation for communication and social awareness appears disrupted in autism.

- By 16 months - Absence of 2-word phrases like "more milk." No pointing or showing things of interest to others. Limited pretend play like feeding dolls or stuffed animals. Neurotypical toddlers this age display primitive language combining words and word-like sounds as they engage in purposeful social communication.

- By 24 months - Any loss of previously acquired speech, babbling or social skills. Trouble switching between activities or tolerating minor changes in routine. Repetitive motions like hand flapping or lining up toys. Poor eye contact and limited interest in peers. By age two, typical children speak in 2-4 word phrases, demonstrate interactive play with imagination, and have an interest in other children. Regression or lack of these expected milestones is cause for immediate evaluation.

Bringing up early concerns empowers your provider to make appropriate referrals for speech, occupational or behavioral therapies to facilitate development. Progress in communication, social and motor domains can then be closely monitored. Early intervention is invaluable in building critical neurological pathways that enable learning. During infancy and toddlerhood, the brain has peak neuroplasticity, so crisis intervention at the first signs of delay gives children the best chance of gaining skills that come less intuitively to them.

Autism involves differences in early brain development that disrupt the acquisition of core abilities in realms like social cognition, communication, behavior regulation and motor planning. As all skills build on each other, prompt treatment fosters foundational capacities to support increasing complexity. Given the life-long impacts, the benefits of early detection and stimulation therapy for autism during ages 0-3 are extraordinarily valuable. Don't hesitate to raise any concerns and advocate persistently for help.

Navigating the Evaluation Process

If screening indicates possible autism, a comprehensive diagnostic evaluation is warranted. The assessment process examines developmental history, observable symptoms, and functional impairments through:

- Parent/caregiver interviews – These involve detailed questions about the child's behaviors, communication, social interactions, play skills, sensory issues, habits and milestones. Tracking specifics to share like when words emerged then stopped, when interest in peers declined, or episodes of hand flapping provides important insights. Any family history of autism or related disorders will also be noted, as there are genetic factors involved.

- Medical history review – Documentation of prenatal, birth and health conditions, physical exam findings, hearing/vision tests and prior evaluations guides the diagnosis. This helps identify any associated conditions. Metabolic disorders, seizures, gastrointestinal disease, sleep abnormalities, immune dysfunction and mental health disorders commonly co-occur with autism.

- Direct structured observation – The child will be observed playing or engaging in various activities to look for social and communication deficits. Repetitive behaviors, sensitivity to stimuli and unusual motor mannerisms will also be noted. Standardized assessment tools like the Autism Diagnostic Observation Schedule (ADOS-2) help quantify and qualify behaviors for diagnostic purposes.

- Standardized autism screening tools – Structured interactive assessments like the ADOS-2, Childhood Autism Rating Scale (CARS) and Social Responsiveness Scale (SRS-2) have clinicians rate the presence and severity of behaviors that align with diagnostic criteria. They measure qualities like eye contact, reciprocity, imaginative play, repetitive actions, sensory responses and peer interactions.

- Cognitive/developmental assessments – Instruments like the Mullen Scales of Early Learning, Vineland Adaptive Behavior Scales, or Bayley Scales of Infant Development evaluate cognitive, speech, motor, socialization and daily living skills. Comparing ability levels in these domains helps identify patterns of strengths and deficits indicating autism.

- Language assessments – Evaluating both expressive and receptive language skills is key in autism diagnosis. Instruments like the Preschool Language Scales (PLS-5) and Clinical Evaluation of Language Fundamentals assess speech, vocabulary, syntax, comprehension and conversational pragmatics.

- Questionnaires – Providers like teachers, therapists and siblings who interact with the child regularly may complete validated questionnaires like the Social Communication Questionnaire (SCQ) or Social Responsiveness Scale (SRS-2) to share observations from multiple environments.

- Play assessments – Unstructured play sessions are filmed to analyze social engagement, shared enjoyment, imagination, role playing and flexibility within play. Rigidity, limited symbolic representation and lack of peers engagement provides clues.

- Sensory assessments – Questionnaires like the Sensory Profile identify atypical reactions to stimuli indicating sensory integration challenges frequently accompanying autism.

- Genetic testing – While identifying genetic mutations associated with autism risk has important research value, it currently has limited clinical utility for most individuals. There are no genetic tests that can definitively diagnose or alter the course of autism itself. Testing for syndromes like Fragile X, RETT, SHANK3, Pitt-Hopkins, Angelman and tuberous sclerosis can sometimes pinpoint genetic abnormalities affecting development. However, altogether these account for only about 10% of autism cases. The genetics and epigenetics of autism are highly complex, with environmental factors also playing a key role. While recognizing genetic contributions, it is important not to get overly focused on this area. Regardless of genetic makeup, much can still be done to improve the child's health, skills and quality of life through biomedical interventions and therapy. Caregivers are encouraged to focus efforts on the aspects of health and development within their control. Identifying and addressing nutritional deficiencies, gut issues, toxic exposures, immune dysregulation, metabolic abnormalities and other biological factors through testing can profoundly help the child reach their potential regardless of genetic status.

- Medical/laboratory tests - Standard bloodwork, urinalysis, EEG, and other biometrics may identify associated conditions like seizures, allergies, nutritional deficiencies, sleep disorders, or gastrointestinal issues that commonly co-occur with autism. However, there are no specific biomarkers that can conclusively diagnose autism itself. Ongoing research seeks to better understand the complex genetic and environmental underpinnings.

After collecting and synthesizing information from all sources, the diagnosis will be determined based on whether the established criteria for Autism Spectrum Disorder are fully met. Key diagnostic aspects include:

- Impairment in social communication and interaction - Deficits in social-emotional reciprocity, reading subtle cues, understanding perspective, forming/maintaining relationships.

- Restricted, repetitive patterns of behavior, activities, or interests – Stereotyped motor mannerisms, inflexible adherence to routines, ritualized patterns of behavior, fixated interests abnormal in focus or intensity.

- Symptom onset during early development – Delays or abnormalities must be present in early childhood, even if subtle or masked by learned coping mechanisms later.

- Clinically significant impairment in function – Difficulties coping with ordinary life situations and demands, leading to reduced independence.

To receive a formal diagnosis of autism spectrum disorder, a child must meet criteria in all these areas. Previous subcategories like Asperger syndrome, pervasive developmental disorder-not otherwise specified (PDD-NOS) and autistic disorder were folded into the umbrella autism spectrum disorder diagnosis in the Diagnostic and Statistical Manual of Mental Disorders 5th edition (DSM-5).

ASD encompasses a wide range of symptom severity. Levels from 1 to 3 help characterize how much support an individual requires related to their communication deficits and restricted/repetitive behaviors:

- Level 1: Requiring support for deficits in social communication and restrictive behaviors.

- Level 2: Requiring substantial support due to impaired verbal and nonverbal skill, limited social engagement, and restrictive/repetitive behaviors that are obvious to casual observers.
- Level 3: Requiring very substantial support for severe deficits in communication skills, flexibility and adapting to change that cause great distress.

Obtaining a thorough diagnostic evaluation from a specialist like a developmental pediatrician, child psychiatrist, neuropsychologist or clinical psychologist with expertise in assessing autism is essential before pursuing intervention services. Educational psychologists can also conduct evaluations required for school services eligibility. Diagnosis should not be rushed; it often requires multiple appointments to complete the full assessment battery.

Throughout the process, parents serve a vital role providing detailed developmental history and advocating for their child's needs every step of the way. Asking questions, taking notes and tracking symptoms at home helps inform clinicians. If any aspects of testing or clinical impressions feel unsatisfactory, seeking a second opinion is perfectly valid. An accurate, well-substantiated diagnosis opens doors to support services and tailoring treatment to maximize outcomes.

Processing an Autism Diagnosis

Even when autism is suspected, having it confirmed can feel like a devastating blow. The grieving process is intense and complex. Common emotions like shock, anger, sorrow, guilt or shame are all normal initially. The vision you had for your child's life may no longer seem possible. Take time to work through this – it's an important part of ultimately coming to acceptance.

Here are some tips that may help in coping with the diagnosis:

- Let yourself fully experience the emotions as they come. Suppressing feelings will only prolong the pain. Confide in trusted loved ones for support. Joining a support group connects you with others navigating the same journey.
- Avoid placing blame on yourself or your parenting. The causes of autism are complex and still not fully understood. Research suggests a combination of genetic, epigenetic and environmental factors outside parental control.
- Gather information to understand your child's challenges and strengths. This knowledge will empower you to be the best advocate and guide your priorities. Educate yourself on the services and therapies available.

- Celebrate small wins and milestones. Focus on the positive moments of connection that make your child special. Recognizing their wonderful personality remains unchanged.

- Be gently patient with yourself. Adjusting outlooks and expectations takes time. Progress through the stages of grief in your own way. You've got this!

- Maintain boundaries around well-meaning advice that leaves you feeling judged or inadequate. Refocus on following your instincts – you know your child best.

- Seek counseling to process painful emotions and gain skills for coping resiliently. A therapist provides objective guidance and support.

- Connect with other families facing similar challenges. Support groups, forums and friends within the autism community provide invaluable understanding and validation. You are not alone.

- Make self-care a priority – proper rest, nutrition, exercise and me-time restores your energy for the journey ahead. Caregiver burnout is real. Support networks and respite care help share the load.

- Focus on each day. Keep perspective by concentrating on the present more than far-off uncertainties. Appreciate every delightful moment with your unique, wonderful child.

With time, information and support, most families adjust well and develop great capacity to nurture their child's growth. Though emotionally taxing at times, the autism journey also offers profound rewards as you gain perspective on what matters most. Your child needs you; by taking good care of yourself, you'll have the strength and resilience to take good care of them.

Patience, flexibility and fierce love for your child will smooth the path ahead.

You've got this!

The path forward has its difficulties, but the bonds formed through compassionately supporting your child's unique needs are truly meaningful. With the proper help, many children make remarkable developmental strides. Stay hopeful!

Chapter 3

Therapies and Interventions

After an autism diagnosis, a key question many parents have is "What treatments will help my child?" There are a variety of behavioral, educational, speech, occupational and complementary therapies that have been shown to improve communication, behavior, self-sufficiency and quality of life. Creating an integrated intervention plan tailored to your child's needs is the key to success.

Overview of Common Therapies

Some of the most widely used and researched autism therapies include:

- **Applied Behavior Analysis (ABA)** – This behavioral treatment uses principles of learning theory to shape behaviors, teach skills and reduce problematic actions. Key techniques like positive reinforcement, modeling, prompting and repeated practice develop communication, social, academic, adaptive and cognitive skills. ABA is highly structured and data-driven, with each session building on the last. It was developed specifically for autism intervention and has the most empirical evidence supporting its effectiveness. ABA is overseen by a Board Certified Behavior Analyst (BCBA) and carried out by Registered Behavior Technicians (RBTs). It can be delivered

1:1 or in small groups. Intensive ABA for multiple years early in life has the best outcomes.

- **Speech Therapy** – Speech-language pathologists address verbal and nonverbal communication deficits in autism. Goals often include improving articulation, building vocabulary and grammar, fostering social language use, developing conversation abilities and teaching use of communication devices. Helping with pragmatic language skills like social cues, figurative speech and reciprocity may be incorporated. Guidance with feeding difficulties related to oral-motor challenges is also provided. Speech therapy typically occurs 1:1 or in small groups, focusing both on structured techniques and facilitating generalizing skills into natural environments.

- **Occupational Therapy (OT)** – Targets fine motor, visual motor and sensorimotor skills involved in functional activities of daily living, play, and schoolwork. Goals include improving grasp, hand-eye coordination, manipulation, handwriting, dressing and other self-care tasks. Addressing sensory processing differences and how to adapt tasks and environments to optimize regulation and engagement is another key focus. Occupational therapy helps adapt skills and tools to enable greater independence. Sessions involve engaging sensory-based activities tailored to the child's needs and interests to develop motor planning.

- **Physical Therapy (PT)** – Develops gross motor skills like balance, strength, coordination and purposeful movement. Gait training, exercises for muscle tone/control and sensory integration activities improve capacities for motions involved in walking, running, jumping and other play or sports. Adapting environments and providing assistive equipment as needed facilitates safety and success. For children struggling with motor skills, PT facilitates active participation and peer interactions critical for social and cognitive growth.

- **Social Skills Training** – Highly structured interventions that use modeling, rehearsing, prompting and coaching to teach appropriate social behavior. Goals include building perspective-taking, reading social cues, practicing conversation skills, developing friendship skills and learning coping strategies for social demands. Role playing and video modeling are often incorporated. Social skills groups provide a natural environment to rehearse these capacities with peers.

- **Cognitive Behavioral Therapy (CBT)** – A structured psychotherapy tailored to children on the spectrum to improve regulation of thoughts, emotions and behavior. Uses positive reinforcement, modeling appropriate responses, social narratives and comic strip conversations to reshape thought patterns. Helps build skills to manage anxiety, reduce disruptive behaviors and stop detrimental thought cycles. Enhances capacity to cope with frustrations and control impulsive reactions. Can be done individually or in groups.

- Sensory Integration Therapy – Uses specialized equipment and activities that provide calming or stimulating input to the various senses – vestibular (balance/motion), proprioceptive (body position), tactile (touch), auditory and visual. Helps adapt responses to sensations and modulate reactions to stimuli that cause dysregulation. Sensory gyms with swings, trampolines, tactile walls, mini climbing structures and more immerse kids in just the right types of input they crave to stay regulated and engaged.

- **Medications** – Pharmaceuticals may be prescribed to curb severe aggressive behavior, improve focus, reduce obsessive behaviors, treat anxiety/depression or regulate brain chemistry shown to be disrupted in autism. Medications like selective serotonin reuptake inhibitors (SSRIs), stimulants, alpha agonists and antipsychotics target neurotransmitter imbalances evidenced biologically. Please be advised to use Ibuprofen instead of Acetaminophen, because the later opens up the brain barrier and can have a significant effect on your child. However, meds should be used cautiously and in conjunction with therapies and counseling. Detailed monitoring for benefits and side effects is essential.

- **Neurofeedback** – Also called EEG biofeedback, this technique uses real-time displays of brain activity to teach self-regulation of brain patterns that are dysfunctional in ASD, like over-arousal. Rewards are given for boosting attention, calmness and executive functions. Some initial studies show improved behavior, communication and quality of life. More research is underway.

- **Assistive Technology** – Electronic devices, software and other tools
  provide helpful supports improving quality of life across settings.
  Communication aids like tablets with speech apps foster interaction.
  Visual schedules, alarms, timers and reminders promote
  organization. Noise-cancelling headphones, weighted blankets and
  fidgets aid self-regulation. Apps offer learning games, video
  modeling and life skills education. Technology removes barriers and
  expands capacities.

Creating an Integrated Intervention Plan

With many possibilities to consider, have your child evaluated by a team of
autism specialists like psychologists, speech pathologists, occupational
therapists and behavioral analysts to determine which therapies should be
priorities. Gaining consensus on the biggest functional issues to target first is
key to coordinating a cohesive treatment plan across domains. Ask each
evaluator to outline specific recommended goals.

Consistency across activities and environments is critical, so choose
providers willing to collaborate on setting objectives, sharing data and
reviewing progress. Request they use compatible behavioral techniques and
terminology. Beware of adding therapies piecemeal without clear purpose.
Too many disjointed interventions risks overloading schedules and slowing
skill development. Carefully consider whether each new service aligns with
priority goals.

Aim for a thoughtful balance of individualized therapies, small interactive groups, and unstructured time for child-led exploration. While structured treatments are beneficial, so is letting kids relax, play imaginatively and just be themselves! Downtime fosters cognitive integration of emerging skills. All learning, no play dulls motivation over time. Monitor stress signals suggesting overscheduling.

Incorporating behavioral modification principles and natural learning opportunities into daily home life is also hugely impactful. For example, use visual schedules, timers, structured choices and clear instructions to provide helpful routines. Practice social scripts before playdates or trips to the store. Provide calming spaces where your child can decompress. Encourage interactive play with siblings. This consistency across environments reinforces new skills. Transfer of knowledge to real world situations is the ultimate goal.

Partnering with Your Child's Team

Active parent involvement with your child's therapists and treatment providers leads to the best outcomes. Here are some tips:

- Learn the terminology, guiding principles and specific techniques being used in sessions. Ask for hands-on training to use these effectively at home. Videos can demonstrate and explain the methods in action.

- Check in regularly about your child's latest progress and ongoing challenges. Share observations and videos from home and jointly problem-solve.

- Request guidance on compassionately handling problem behaviors and meltdowns to keep everyone safe. Discuss triggers to avoid and productive responses. Access crisis intervention if needed.

- Speak up if certain therapies seem ineffective after an adequate trial or if any concerning new behaviors emerge. Be willing to tweak techniques or shift gears.

- Share what motivates your child - preferred activities, high interest topics, powerful reinforcers - so these can be naturally incorporated into teaching.

- Celebrate both big milestone achievements and small steps forward! Recognizing incremental progress boosts motivation and confidence to build new skills.

Ask for training on how to foster target skills during daily routines like dressing, meals, errands, and play. Generalization is key.

By educating yourself on autism and your child's treatments, communicating frequently, and actively supporting the therapies, you become an empowered member of the care team. Your daily observations and insights are invaluable for tailoring the interventions to achieve success. Stay engaged.

Navigating Financial Aspects of Treatment

Understand your insurance benefits and network providers. But know many effective biomed treatments and specialty tests will be out-of-pocket. Saving accounts like HSAs help offset these costs.

- While basic autism therapies may be covered, accessing renowned specialists in the field often requires self-pay. The best doctors have long waitlists and require prepaid deposits for telemedicine or in-person visits.
- For example, our family paid $700 out-of-pocket for an initial consultation with a leading pediatric neurologist in Connecticut. Follow-ups are $250. His expertise has been invaluable, but such costs are common.
- You will likely need to travel out-of-state to find doctors on the cutting edge of testing and treating autism. Our specialists have been in Nevada, Florida, New York, and Canada. We live in Tennessee.
- Many supplements and compounded medications these practitioners recommend are also not covered by insurance. We easily spend $300/month on supplements, enzymes, vitamins, and amino acids.
- DAN (Defeat Autism Now) doctors, MAPS practitioners, and clinicians trained by The Medical Academy of Pediatric Special Needs use

intensive biomed approaches that yield real improvements, but at
substantial self-pay costs.

- If finances are limiting access to optimal care, look into grants from
  autism foundations, Medicaid waivers, state disability services, travel
  assistance programs, and non-profits. Crowdfunding campaigns are
  also an option.

- Save all receipts. Categorize medical vs educational expenses.
  Accountants can help maximize tax deductions, credits and FSAs. But
  assume you'll pay out-of-pocket for your child's best chance at
  progress. It's a worthwhile investment.

- Be cautious of excessive therapies. Focus on quality over quantity. As
  skills improve, service hours can often be reduced or refocused.
  Don't automatically renew long-term therapy contracts.

The road to helping your child reach their potential may be expensive. But
specialized testing and care from the best doctors produces real
improvements in skills, health and quality of life that are priceless. Prioritize
what's truly needed. With smart financial planning, you can secure the ideal
care.

Advocating for Your Child's Needs

Pursuing the best possible therapies, school supports and medical care for an autistic child often requires assertiveness and perseverance. You may need to:

- Appeal to insurance to cover evidence-based autism therapies. Cite established benefits, laws requiring coverage, and deny denials. File complaints with state regulators regarding parity violations.

- Educate school staff on recommended learning accommodations and modifications to support your child. Provide evaluation reports clarifying challenges. Send follow-up letters confirming meetings. Learn the system's jargon.

- Ask providers for a written treatment plan listing specific goals so services remain coordinated and focused. Request regular progress reports. Update goals as mastery is achieved.

- Obtain referrals to needed specialists like neurologists, psychiatrists, gastroenterologists, immunologists, allergists or nutritionists to evaluate medical aspects and treat comorbidities.

- Tour potential schools and programs to find the best match for your child's learning style, skills and sensitivities. Ask about ratios, therapies, inclusion models and past outcomes. Observe classes.

- Connect with autism advocacy groups for guidance navigating systems. They offer practical advice, Legal resources, and peer support. Sometimes formally lodging complaints is needed to instigate change.

The process can feel daunting but persist. Speaking up empowers you to secure the services your child needs to keep developing skills for an independent, fulfilled life. You are their voice. With your unwavering love and advocacy, they can continue making strides toward a bright future. Your determination and hope fuels their potential.

Chapter 4

Communication and Social Skills

Because autism is characterized by challenges in social communication and interaction, targeting deficits in these realms is essential to helping children reach their full potential. This chapter covers strategies parents can use at home to nurture their child's communication abilities, explicitly teach social skills, and help them better navigate interpersonal interactions.

Building Communication Skills

Spoken language development is often significantly delayed or impaired in children on the autism spectrum. Many remain minimally verbal or nonverbal. Even those who gain phrase speech tend to have ongoing difficulties with reciprocal conversation, abstract language, figurative meanings and nonverbal cues that unwritten social communication rules rely upon.

However, tailored interventions can help develop verbal and nonverbal communication capacities to whatever extent possible for the individual child. It simply takes creativity, patience and meeting them at their developmental level. Teaching communication is deeply rewarding as skills unfold – verbal or nonverbal. The motivation to connect is what matters most.

Strategies for Emerging Communicators

For children at early pre-verbal or limited verbal stages, focus on building blocks like joint attention, turn-taking, following simple directions and expressing basic wants and needs through any modality.

- Respond to and reinforce all attempts to communicate, whether through vocalizations, gestures, pictures, signs, sounds or eye contact. Interpret cues, provide models for using words, and celebrate progress.
- Use picture exchange systems like PECS to teach functionally requesting items, activities and needs from a communication partner by handing them a relevant picture or pressing icons on a speech device. This shows the pictures represent something meaningful.
- Incorporate tablets, voice output devices like GoTalk buttons, and sign language to supplement or augment verbal language. These aids allow nonverbal children to actively participate in communication exchanges. High-tech augmentative communication devices can be introduced too. Choices provide a sense of control.
- Try iconic word charts, visual aids, objects, tactile symbols, written words, Braille, and calendar boxes as helpful tools depending on the child's abilities. Remove reliance on just speech.

- Simplify multi-step instructions into smaller chunks. Use visual supports like picture sequences. Allow extra processing time. Check for comprehension - don't assume.

- Describe your actions, the surrounding environment, routines and emotions out loud. This exposes children to vocabulary, sentence structure and narrative discourse patterns.

- Have child echo or imitate your gestures, sounds, and facial expressions. Clap syllables in words together, tap out rhythms and stress tones.

- Read interactive picture books encouraging participation like lifting flaps, pointing, making sounds.

For more verbal communicators:

As phrase speech emerges, maintaining momentum with continued speech therapy facilitates building sentences, conversation abilities, vocabulary and language interpretation.

- Have frequent back-and-forth exchanges centered around your child's interests to keep practicing initiating, responding, turn taking and maintaining shared focus. Model good reciprocity.

- Ask them to relay stories, describe events, explain things they know a lot about, and share opinions. Gently prompt for key details they miss and appropriate eye contact.

- Work on speaking at an appropriate pace and volume with proper phrasing, emphasis and inflection. Have them repeat target words and phrases while you model. Songs also build prosody.
- Practice strategies for repairing communication breakdowns or misunderstandings. Provide scripts explaining they did not understand or requesting clarification.
- Expose your child to figurative language like idioms, sarcasm, metaphors and nuanced meanings that tend to confuse literal autistic thinkers. Act out idioms. Explain nonliteral phrases.
- Expand vocabulary knowledge through reading together, word games, flashcards and language activities. Write out word webs together.
- Work on grammar skills like using pronouns properly, subject-verb agreement, tense consistency and sentence structure.
- Practice perspective-taking and viewing situations from others' point of view. Pose "what if" scenarios.

Other general communication strategies:

- Avoid overloading your child with complex verbal instructions or rapid-fire questions. Pause, allow ample processing time. Break communication down into smaller digestible chunks.
- Alternate activities with high language demands with calmer periods. Monitor for signs of overload like stimming or tantrums.
- Narrate your actions, thoughts and feelings out loud to provide a continual model of functional communication. Describe emotions you observe others experiencing.

- Encourage nonverbal listening skills like appropriate eye gaze, nodding along, and facial expressions conveying empathy. Teach reading body language cues in conversations.

- Personalize the environment with vocabulary flashcards, alphabet strips, printed schedules, and visual supports. Surround children with language.

- Seek speech-language therapy focusing both on structured techniques and generalizing skills into natural daily environments. Consistency across settings cultivates lasting abilities.

- Celebrate all attempts to interact with words, signs or pictures! The desire to connect is what matters most. Meet children at their communication level.

Explaining and Social Thinking

Many social interaction skills we naturally absorb from observing others do not come easily for autistic children without explicit teaching. But social expectations, hidden curriculum, and unwritten "rules" of interpersonal engagement can be broken down through direct instruction, modeling, rehearsal and gentle coaching. Target key skills like:

- Making appropriate eye contact during interactions vs avoiding gazes. Use photos of faces and emoji faces to demonstrate looks conveying different emotions.

- Practicing common polite greetings and conversational skills like taking turns, listening without interrupting, asking relevant questions or building on what others say. Role play scenarios.

- Learning about personal space boundaries and appropriate physical touch. Use tape outlines, hula hoops or furniture to define individual spaces. Demonstrate asking before hugging.

- Recognizing causes of emotions in characters while reading books or watching shows together. Pick up on context clues. Discuss compassionate ways to show concern for others' feelings.

- Taking others' perspectives - explain how one situation could make different people feel different emotions based on their thoughts, personality and past experiences.

- Regulating one's own emotions and controlling impulses that affect social responses. Teach calming techniques, walking away when upset and asking for a break.

- Building friendships - coach on how to approach others, suggest play ideas, cope with conflicts and rejection. Explain compromising.

Other helpful social learning strategies include:

- Social narratives and scripts that demonstrate expected behavior in various contexts - school, restaurants, playgrounds, playdates, parties, etc. Personalize stories with the child's interests.

- Video modeling that shows peers appropriately demonstrating target skills. Pausing to discuss and practice key steps cements learning.

- Social skills groups that allow guided rehearsal of conversational skills, cooperation, turn-taking and coping with peer dynamics in a small supportive environment.
- Visual aids like emotion charts and sequence steps for proper greetings, taking turns, listening and reciprocity. Make the implicit explicit.
- Behavior reward systems that reinforce positive social responses and redirect negative reactions. Use motivating rewards.

With time, consistency, and scaffolded support, children can practice social skills until they become more habitual and generalize to other contexts. What seems innate for neurotypical children can be deliberately taught to children on the spectrum. Supporting success in social realms vastly improves quality of life.

Navigating Interpersonal Situations

The unpredictability and fluid nature of real-world social situations can seem overwhelming. Help foster successful interactions by:

- Providing visual schedules, social scripts or stories explaining in concrete terms what will happen, who will be there, what they may do or say. Reduces uncertainty.
- Coaching them on potential conversation topics, appropriate questions to ask about others, and things they could share about themselves or their interests. Brainstorm possibilities.

- Practicing likely scenarios ahead of time through role play like losing a game gracefully, compromising on what to play, or negotiating taking turns. Talk through appropriate responses.

- Creating a safe "break space" they can retreat to independently if feeling overwhelmed. Carrying a picture of the quiet space helps. Process the experience together afterward.

- Debriefing social encounters as a learning opportunity - what went well? Did any problems occur, and how could they be handled differently next time?

- Sharing strategies for coping with teasing, exclusion or rejection. Discuss talking to a teacher, trusted adult, or coming up with an assertive response.

- Reminding them of their inner strengths, talents, and qualities so they know their value. Build resilience.

With preparation, guidance and compassion, children can gain confidence interacting and forging meaningful social connections. Though it takes time, patience and repetition, the rewards of seeing social awareness blossom are incredibly fulfilling. Meet them where they are developmentally, appreciate small wins, and keep focusing on moving forward.

Encouraging Functional Communication at Home

Creating a communication-rich home environment tailored to your child's abilities sets them up for ongoing growth. Incorporate these tips:

Augmentative & Alternative Communication (AAC):

- If your child is nonverbal, consult speech pathologists about appropriate low-tech and high-tech AAC options to supplement speech. These tools allow functional communication and greater independence no matter the verbal ability.

- Low-tech aids like picture exchange boards, choice boards with velcro symbols, alphabet flip-books, word walls, and voice output switches and buttons can be introduced as early as 12 months. Select images that most motivate your child.

- High-tech voice output communication devices like GoTalk, NovaChat, ProLoQuo2Go, LAMP Words for Life, and TapToTalk provide text-to-speech features for more complex messaging. These build toward more advanced aug-com devices.

- Apps like Proloquo4Text put robust communication support at one's fingertips. The iPad's cool factor and ease of use appeals to kids. Portability fosters wider social connections.

- Ensure family members, teachers, therapists, and peers learn to use the child's AAC system to model effective communication exchanges and prompt expanded messages. Using their preferred modality builds confidence and skills.

Visual Supports:

- Creative use of photos, icons, drawings, lists, bulletin boards, posters schedules, calendars, charts, webs, and timelines provides helpful visual structure and cues throughout the home.

- Picture activity schedules, first-then boards, choice boards, mini schedules on keyrings, and social stories displayed with velcro give a sense of reassuring routine and sequence.

- Label favorite objects, spaces, bins and baskets with picture icons, words or both to build word-referent connections and promote independence.

- Dry erase boards provide a fun, simple way to draw or write choices, steps of a routine, conversation topics, and more to make verbal information more concrete.

Language Exposure & Growth:

- Surround your child with domain-specific word walls – favorite foods, animals, hobbies, places – with real photos or magazine cut outs. Engage them in categorizing words together.

- Read aloud together often – print awareness skills precede reading skills. Discuss new vocabulary in lively ways. Emphasize how words connect to relevant experiences.

- Similarly discuss new words that come up throughout your days together – errands, car rides, play. Synonym and antonym activities build depths of meaning.

- Speech-language apps provide engaging ways to target articulation, descriptive language, wh- questions, categorization and other goals through games and visual formats.

- Singing builds speech rhythm, inflection, syllables and vocabulary too. Nursery rhymes, silly songs and upbeat movement songs incentivize vocal play.

No matter your child's verbal abilities, dedicating focused time to communicating each day in ways that make sense to them pays invaluable dividends in fostering interaction, comprehension, shared enjoyment and quality of life.

Chapter 5

Sensory Processing Challenges in Autism

Up to 90% of people with autism have some degree of sensory processing dysfunction. This means they have trouble taking in, organizing and responding appropriately to input from the seven senses: sight, hearing, smell, taste, touch, vestibular (motion/balance) and proprioception (body awareness). Given how pervasive sensory experiences are, addressing these difficulties can dramatically improve children's behavior, emotional regulation, focus, and participation in daily life activities.

Understanding Sensory Dysfunction

Those with sensory processing disorders misinterpret everyday sensory information in a way that interferes with learning, relationships, coordination and adaptive responses. Sensory signals either get intensified resulting in sensory overload, or inadequately registered leading to sensory seeking behaviors to stimulate more input.

Sensory overload – Being overly sensitive to certain stimuli. Reactions signaling overload include:

- Covering ears or appearing pained by noises like vacuum cleaners, crowd chatter, music, car horns or even loud voices

- Wincing at or avoiding bright or flickering lights, visual clutter, colorful patterns, shapes or excessive movement

- Refusing to walk barefoot on grass, sand or textured surfaces. Disliking certain food textures and temperatures. Gagging at smells.

- Crying, pulling away or lashing out when touched unexpectedly. Disliking hugs, affection, having hair brushed or face washed.

- Being distressed by clothes with scratchy tags, seams or tight elastic bands. Needing to wear same soft clothes.

- Avoiding activities like climbing or amusement park rides. Fearful when feet leave the ground.

Sensory seeking – Craving extra sensory input. Often involves:

- Repeatedly touching, licking, tapping, scratching or squeezing objects. Mouthing non-food items past typical oral exploration age.

- Intense fascination with lights, reflections, water, sand, or items with mechanisms that spin or open/close like doors, toy car wheels or washing machines.

- Excessive sniffing or staring intently at objects, textures, movements or lights. Visually inspecting people's faces up close.

- Chewing on shirt collars, sleeves or other clothing items. Eating non-edible substances like dirt or chalk.

- Fascination with textures like dripping water, slime, playdough, or finger painting. Craving messy hands-on play.

- Unusually high pain tolerance - lack of response to major injuries. Roughhousing and deep pressure.

- Love of jumping, bumping, pushing, wrestling, stomping. Seeking fast/spinning carnival rides.

The type and degree of sensory dysfunction varies widely among individuals. Some have mild differences in one or two senses, while others experience profound challenges across multiple domains. Symptoms may also fluctuate in severity at different ages or stages due to factors like health, environment, routines and communication skills. Paying attention to your child's unique sensitivities is key to providing effective supports.

Creating a Sensory Friendly Home Environment

You can make adaptations to your home and daily schedule to help accommodate your child's needs:

Physical Spaces:

- Reduce visual and auditory clutter where possible. Soothing paint colors like light blue or gray on walls are calming backdrops. Natural lighting is gentler.
- Window treatments like blackout curtains and blinds help control brightness and glare. Rugs absorb sound and echo. White noise machines add pleasant background sensory input.

- Store toys/supplies out of sight in bins, baskets or closets when not in use. Rotate just a few preferred items at a time. Too much visual input is overwhelming.

- Incorporate cozy spaces for retreating when overloaded – tents, cushy beanbag chairs or floor mattresses in a corner, play houses, lofts. Use soundproofing panels, low lighting, soft pillows and blankets. Allow sensory toys and headphones.

- Outdoor areas like yards, patios or balconies make great movement spaces for running, jumping, spinning when active sensory input is craved. Have a variety of balls, bubbles, sidewalk chalk, and toys for water play.

Transitions and Schedules:

- Prepare for transitions between activities and settings using visual aids like picture schedules, timers, alarms, and count-downs. Verbally warn of coming changes. Limit waiting when possible – it's agonizing.

- Build in extra time for transitions in daily routines like getting dressed, driving places, entering/leaving school. Prevent feeling rushed.

- Use consistent schedules and routines where possible to promote a sense of safety and predictability. Mark favorite parts of the day like playtime or snack visually.

Regulation Tools:

- Have preferred sensory items readily available to provide organizing input – tactile/fidget toys, resistance bands, trampolines, swings, vibrating cushions, weighted blankets. Offer these as soon as stress signals appear.

- Sunglasses, brimmed caps, earmuffs and noise-cancelling headphones allow control over incoming visual and auditory input. Some public places like airports have "sensory kits" to borrow.

- Keep preferred snacks on hand. Chewing and the flavors/textures of crunchy or sour foods can have regulating effects.

- Allow access to preferred music for auditory stimulation. Loud rhythmic music is energizing, while soft melodic music is soothing.

Preparing for Challenging Events:

- For errands, social gatherings, restaurants or travel, preview plans using social scripts, picture stories or lists detailing what comes next, who will be there, what sensory experiences to expect. Verbal warnings help, but visuals make the unfamiliar more concrete and predictable. Ask teachers for classroom social stories you can reference.

- Pack portable sensory supports like headphones, sunglasses, fidgets, weighted lap pads, snacks, music players. Having toolkits with personalized comforting and alerting items provides security.

- Go over strategies ahead of time for asking for breaks, speaking up about discomfort, or retreating to a quiet corner. Agree on special

cues or signals your child can use if feeling overwhelmed or
overstimulated.

Responding to Sensory Meltdowns

When children become overtaxed by sensory stimuli, painful behavioral
outbursts or meltdowns often occur as a fight-flight-freeze response.
Strategies to compassionately deescalate and recover:

- Remain calm yourself – Speak gently in simple phrases. Use their
  name. Model slow deep breathing. Overreacting with anger or
  threats makes things worse.
- Remove from triggers – Guide them to a quieter space with
  carpeting, beanbags or mats. Offer noise-cancelling headphones if
  sound sensitivity triggered upset. Provide preferred objects to hold
  and manipulate.
- Offer organizing sensory input to counteract chaos – Wrap in a
  weighted blanket, gently rock or massage, turn down lights, play
  ambient music, provide compression.
- Teach self-regulation – With time, they can learn to self-identify
  warning signs of distress and use coping techniques like asking for
  breaks, deep breathing, or retreating to sensory-friendly spaces.
- Allow recovery time after meltdowns to recharge without interaction
  demands or distractions. Children often need to fully reconnect with
  their senses before resuming tasks. Quiet reflection helps process
  emotions and problem-solve triggers.

- When ready, gently help identify what overwhelmed them, rehearse calmer responses, then transition back into activities. End interactions on a positive note – the goal is reducing shame and building skills over time, not punishment.

Preparing for stimulating events, responding patiently in the moment, then compassionately processing experiences afterward helps reduce the severity and frequency of sensory-triggered meltdowns over time. Your support makes all the difference in building sensory regulation skills.

Exploring Sensory Integration Therapy

Occupational therapists (OTs) who pursue advanced certification in this specialized approach use sensory-based activities to help children better modulate, process, and respond to sensory information. Goals of sensory integration therapy include:

- Increasing body awareness and attention to important sensory input
- Promoting appropriate levels of alertness, attention and focus during tasks
- Building motor planning and coordination skills
- Reducing fearful reactions to ordinary sounds, textures, touch or movement
- Decreasing related impulse behaviors and aggression
- Fostering emotional regulation, confidence, and participation

The therapist provides playful activities that stimulate the various sensory systems in ways the child finds organizing and regulating:

Vestibular – Swinging, rocking chairs, sit-n-spin toys, trampolines, rocker boards, scooter boards, hanging equipment. These activate the vestibular system giving calming proprioceptive input.

Proprioceptive – Obstacle courses, trapeze swings, mini climbing walls, tunnel mazes, weighted blankets, resistance bands, jumping, pulling, and deep pressure. Proprioceptive input helps develop body awareness.

Tactile – Finger painting, water play, kinetic sand, playdough, goop, shaving cream, rice bins, massage. These stimulate the tactile system and tactile discrimination.

Visual – Light tables, fiber optic toys, infinity mirrors. These provide mesmerizing visual input that can be either calming or alerting.

Auditory – Instruments, rhythmic toys, rain sticks, music. Sound and vibrations stimulate the auditory system. Calming music soothes, lively music energizes.

Oral/Olfactory – Whistles, bubble blowers, chewing tools, scented items. These stimulate the mouth and nose areas.

The child chooses and directs different sensory activities while the therapist challenges their flexibility by dynamically adjusting these to provide both alerting and calming input. With guidance, the child learns to use sensory tools independently to meet their needs. Over time, improved sensory processing allows greater success with focus, behavior, motor skills and participation across settings.

Sensory diets extending these therapies into daily life are also created. In addition to professional support, simple sensory play at home fosters progress. Examples include hiding small toys in putty or playdough, using spray bottles for water play, making "squish bags" with hair gel and glitter, blowing bubbles, finger painting, or setting up obstacle courses. Focus on keeping activities child-led and infused with fun!

Seeking Solutions

While sensory struggles pose many frustrations, targeted therapies and compassionate support systems help children build resilience. Though sensory difficulties may not fully resolve, progress is always possible. Your understanding of their experiences, advocacy addressing sensitivities, and implementing accommodations makes a major difference in easing distresses so they can feel safe, valued and confident to flourish.

Chapter 6

Behavioral and Emotional Challenges in Autism

Autism is a neurodevelopmental disorder characterized by challenges with social communication and restricted, repetitive behaviors. Many autistic children also struggle significantly with regulating their actions, emotions, and sensory systems. Difficulty communicating needs, coping with change, managing frustration, and modulating responses to stimuli can manifest in a variety of behavioral challenges that impact quality of life.

While problematic behaviors arise for complex reasons, they are not intentional misbehaviors, but rather reflect skills deficits in areas like comprehension, communication, cognition and self-regulation. With compassion, consistency and coaching in lacking skills, children can learn to manage emotions, control actions, and gain confidence. This chapter will expand on common behavioral challenges seen in autism, factors that drive them, and strategies parents can use to support positive behavior in their child.

Common Behavioral Manifestations

Parents may observe a range of behaviors in their autistic child tied to regulation difficulties:

Tantrums and Meltdowns - Intense, lengthy episodes of emotional distress involving crying, screaming, kicking, hitting or biting oneself. Often triggered by frustration with a request or activity, changes in routine, transitions between tasks or settings, too much stimulation, or inability to communicate needs. Meltdowns reflect a temporary loss of behavioral control due to feeling overwhelmed.

Aggression and Self-Injury - Lashing out either toward others or themselves during periods of significant distress. May involve behaviors like hitting, punching, scratching, biting, head banging, picking skin, pulling hair, or hitting oneself. Caused by an overwhelmed sensory system and inability to control escalating emotions. Possibly an attempt to communicate or cope with internal pain.

Rigid Habits and Perseveration - Insistence on set routines or rituals, great distress when they are disrupted, and difficulty with transitions. Frequent repetitive body motions like hand flapping, spinning, pacing, jumping, finger movements. Fixation on certain objects, topics or activities of interest. Difficulty when redirected. Reflects a desire for sameness and sensory-stimulating movement.

Impulsivity and Hyperactivity - Difficulty controlling impulses that result in behaviors like grabbing items without asking, running or pacing about, interrupting conversations or shouting thoughts, or quickly shifting activities. Reflects disinhibition and excessive motor activity. Poses safety risks.

Noncompliance - Disregard for rules, norms, instructions or expectations. May be passive noncompliance like ignoring instructions, avoiding work or hiding, or active defiance like arguing, yelling or throwing. Often tied to deficits in comprehension, communication, memory and motivation.

Poor Focus and Distractibility - Easily distracted by sights, sounds, smells or own thoughts. Difficulty sustaining attention to complete tasks and activities. Prone to restlessness, fidgeting with items and shifting position. Symptoms of weak executive functioning skills.

Anxiety and Withdrawal - Excessive fear, avoidance, clinging, crying or tantrums in social situations, crowded/loud settings or when faced with new activities. May retreat inward due to feeling overwhelmed by stimuli and interactions. Reflects inability to cope with uncertainty.

Underlying Factors Driving Challenging Behaviors

To develop effective supports, it is crucial to understand factors that commonly trigger and maintain problematic behaviors:

- Communication challenges - Difficulty expressing needs, wants, pain, confusion etc. verbally leads to use of behaviors to communicate distress.

- Cognitive rigidity - Insistence on set routines and difficulty coping with transition and unpredictability. Need for control and order.
- Sensory dysregulation - Hyper/hypo-reactivity to sounds, touch, visuals makes regulating reactions and emotions difficult. Easily overwhelmed.
- Motor difficulties - Poor coordination or hyperactivity makes participating in tasks and play difficult, leading to frustration.
- Skill deficits - Struggles with social skills, emotional literacy, coping strategies, problem-solving, etc. impede independence.
- Comprehension deficits - Difficulty understanding spoken/written direction and expectations leads to noncompliance and mistakes.
- Anxiety - Change, uncertainty and overstimulation commonly provoke intense unease, fear, avoidance and meltdowns.
- Poor impulse control - Difficulty self-regulating behavior and emotional reactions due to deficits in executive functioning.
- Medication effects - Side effects of certain medications can exacerbate attention, anxiety, agitation or hyperactivity symptoms.
- Mental health issues - Conditions like anxiety, depression or obsessive compulsive disorder may develop and require treatment.
- Pain/discomfort - Headaches, gut pain, sinus issues, allergies, menstrual cramps, injury or illness can increase irritability.
- Fatigue and hunger - Becoming overly tired or hungry can rapidly reduce coping abilities and spur outbursts.

In most cases, challenging behaviors are not willful, but rather represent neurologically-based struggles with skills like communicating, adapting, focusing, comprehending social norms, sensory modulation and coping with distress. Behaviors often serve a purpose in allowing the child to express pain, avoid demands, get needs met, release anxiety or stimulate their senses.

Developing Proactive Behavioral Supports

The primary goals of intervention are to prevent problematic behaviors by proactively addressing triggering factors in the environment, interactions and skill deficits, as well as teach new behavioral regulation skills. Key principles include:

- Maintain an organized, structured environment with consistent routines and expectations. Prepare for any changes.
- Set up visual schedules, timers, calendars and checklists to provide clarity and predictability.
- Offer choices to increase sense of autonomy and control. Provide frequent sensory and movement breaks.
- Notice and reinforce desired behaviors more than scolding undesired ones. Praise should outnumber corrections.
- Determine appropriate motivators. Tangible rewards, social praise and preferred activities incentivize learning.
- Teach missing social, communication, self-help and coping skills through modeling, practice and role-play.
- Provide accommodations like noise-canceling headphones, sunglasses or fidget toys to aid self-regulation.

- Learn to read your child's signals and intervene at first signs of
  distress to prevent escalation.

- Keep setting, social interactions and requests simple to avoid
  confusion and overload. Give one step directions.

- Debrief challenging incidents calmly once resolved to identify
  triggers and determine better responses.

- Focus on your child's strengths and uniqueness. All behavior has
  meaning and is goal-oriented.

Professional input from licensed behavior analysts, psychologists, occupational therapists, speech therapists and special educators is key for designing an individualized behavior plan tailored to your child's challenges and assets. Input should be sought if self-harm, high intensity aggression or dangerous behaviors emerge. Treatment may involve structured behavioral therapies, social skills training, medications, and family counseling. Consistency between home, school and community maximizes progress.

Structuring the Physical Environment

Structuring the physical environment can be helpful in minimizing triggers and supporting self-regulation. Strategies include:

- Arrange furnishings/play areas to delineate activity spaces and
  delineate room purposes visually.

- Ensure adequate storage to maintain organization of environments
  and materials. Use bins, baskets and labels.

- Select simple, sturdy furnishings that are water/stain resistant and comfortable.

- Reduce clutter and decorative items that may distract. Avoid noisy lighting like fluorescent.

- Set up individual workstations for independent task focus if needed. Use screens/curtains to partition.

- Display visual schedules, calendars, timers and checklists to clarify expectations.

- Play calming music and use diffused lighting to create a relaxing atmosphere.

- Establish clear sensory-friendly spaces for taking movement and emotional breaks when feeling distressed. Provide seating, weighted blankets, fidgets, headphones, soft lighting, etc.

Teaching Replacement Behaviors and Skills

Problematic behaviors often arise from lagging skills and serve a purpose for the child in communicating, coping or self-stimulating. Teaching replacement behaviors through modeling, visual supports and reinforcement can meet the child's needs more appropriately. Focus areas include:

Communication - Build expressive communication skills and provide alternative augmentative communication aids. Teach requesting help, expressing feelings verbally, making choices.

Coping - Brainstorm appropriate strategies for anxiety, disappointment, frustration etc. Practice deep breathing, visualization, exercise, sensory integration tools.

Social Skills - Role play skills like compromising, cooperation, sharing through games and activities. Hold social behavioral therapy groups.

Problem Solving - Generate alternative solutions to difficulties. Learn to alter behavior based on context and environment.

Emotional Literacy - Use stories, games and discussion to understand own and others' feelings. Improves empathy.

Self-Awareness - Connect behaviors and emotions to physical sensations and triggers. Practice reading body signals and articulating needs.

Self-Stimulation - Redirect repetitive behaviors to sensory substitutes like fidget spinners, exercise, music, weighted blankets.

The key is linking behaviors to their function, then teaching and reinforcing an appropriate replacement that meets the child's goal, whether it be sensory stimulation, communication, self-soothing, expressing a need or interacting socially. Start small, shape behaviors through reward systems, and embed practice in everyday activities to promote generalization.

Building Emotional Regulation Skills

Supporting emotional regulation involves teaching children to recognize feelings in themselves and others, articulate needs, tolerate distress, initiate self-soothing, and exert behavioral control. Useful strategies include:

- Provide labels for emotions as they occur. Relate feelings to facial expressions and body cues to build emotional literacy.

- Read stories featuring characters experiencing different feelings. Discuss causes and ways to cope. Role play scenarios.

- Explore strong emotions through art, music and movement activities. Allow safe expression.

- Develop a calming toolkit of preferred fidget toys, headphones, blanket, sunglasses, snacks, music playlist, stuffed animal, bubbles, etc. as self-regulation aids.

- Practice personalized strategies like deep breathing, visualization, meditation, exercise, positive self-talk scripts, humor. Integrate into daily routines.

- Gradually increase coping with non-preferred activities and changes to routines to build tolerance. Offer preferred rewards after.

- Model thinking through problems, setting/achieving goals, overcoming obstacles and regulating reactions. Describe steps out loud.

- Establish a safe space they can independently retreat to when emotions begin escalating. Staff should be nearby to coach through gaining control.

- Notice and praise every attempt at emotional regulation, no matter how small. Progress takes time, effort and consistency.

With modeling, accommodation and opportunities for structured practice, emotional regulation skills can be strengthened. Parents can foster these abilities by remaining calm and emotionally controlled themselves, verbalizing their own feelings and coping methods, empathizing with the child's emotions, and guiding them through the process of achieving mastery over behavioral reactions. Consistency is key as it can take months or more of practice before strategies are internalized and applied independently.

Promoting Positive Behaviors

All behavior serves a purpose and parents should take a compassionate, detective-like approach to discern their child's unique needs and motivators to shape behaviors positively. Strategies include:

- Observe and record behaviors to identify patterns, triggers and functions. Keep tracking data to measure progress.
- Notice and praise positive behaviors frequently, especially replacement skills being taught. Children crave attention, even negative - ensure positives outweigh corrections.
- Let natural consequences do the teaching. E.g. If a toy is thrown, it gets put away for the day. Follow through consistently.
- Provide choice to increase autonomy. Offer two options you find acceptable, then let them choose.

- Use a token reward system. Tokens are earned for exhibiting desired behaviors and traded in for prize after earning set amount. Focuses on positives.

- Catch them being good. Look for and reinforce even small steps in the right direction. Progress takes time.

- Avoid emotional reactions to misbehavior. Respond calmly and impose consequences fairly. Don't discipline out of anger or frustration.

- Maintain realistic expectations based on their developmental level. Accommodate their needs.

- Involve your child in problem solving. Discuss rules and why they exist. Collaborate on solutions.

- Be consistent. Establish routines, model desired responses, communicate expectations clearly and reinforce consistently.

- Focus on strengths and capabilities vs deficits. All children wish to learn, engage and succeed.

With a nurturing, structured approach that plays to their abilities and motivations, problematic behaviors can be reduced as regulation, communication and coping skills grow. Expect setbacks during periods of stress or transition, and respond patiently. Progress takes time but your support and consistency will help your child build lifelong regulation skills.

Chapter 7

Promoting Healthy Sleep in Autism

Sleep issues are very prevalent in autistic children, reported in 50-80% of cases. Difficulties falling asleep, frequent night wakings, early morning risings and poor sleep quality can greatly impact health, development, behavior and quality of life. Establishing soothing bedtime routines, addressing any underlying issues, and teaching self-regulation skills are important for the whole family's wellbeing.

Common Sleep Problems

Parents may observe an array of sleep disturbances, including:

- Bedtime Resistance - Stress settling down to sleep, tantrums or stalling. Racing thoughts, anxiety and overstimulation can prevent unwinding.

- Sleep Onset Delay - Takes an excessively long time to fall asleep once put to bed, often over 60 minutes. Requires parental help to settle.

- Frequent Night Waking - Waking 3+ times per night and requiring caregiver intervention to return to sleep. Disrupts sleep cycles from deepening.

- Early Morning Waking - Waking very early, before parents, and inability to fall back asleep. Leads to daytime fatigue.

- Irregular Sleep Patterns - Inconsistent bedtimes and wake times day to day. Makes establishing healthy circadian rhythms difficult.

- Restless Sleep - Frequent shifting, covers falling off, talking/yelling out indicates inability to sustain deep NREM and REM sleep.

- Nightmares and Night Terrors - Frightening dreams or screams/confusion arousing from deep sleep. Poor sleep quality even if sleep duration is adequate.

- Sleepwalking - Rising from bed and walking about while still asleep. Can prompt safety concerns.

- Sleep Apnea - Breathing pauses during sleep due to airway issues. Impairs oxygenation, continuity and depth of sleep. Screening is recommended.

- Restless Leg Syndrome - Uncomfortable tingling sensations in legs that create urge to move them. Tied to low iron and genetics.

- Delayed Sleep Phase - Circadian rhythm shifted to fall asleep and wake later than normal times. Drives misalignment with school/work demands.

- Insomnia - Habitual difficulty falling or staying asleep. Mental and physical health suffer without restorative sleep.

Contributing Factors

Sleep troubles in autism arise for varied reasons including:

- Communication deficits make it hard to express needs, pains or anxieties keeping them up.

- Hyperactivity, restless legs, tics and caregiver dependence lead to frequent waking.

- Anxiety about sleep itself or next day activities makes unwinding difficult.
- Sensory sensitivities mean normal home noises disturb, prompting light sleep.
- Weak self-regulation skills inhibit ability to self-soothe and modulate reactions that interrupt sleep.
- Insistence on sameness and dependence on bedtime ritual prompts anxiety if disrupted.
- Biological deficits in melatonin production, serotonin circuits, or circadian genes drive irregular sleep cycles.
- Gastrointestinal discomfort from reflux, constipation or food sensitivities may wake them.
- Side effects of medications, like stimulants for ADHD or SSRIs for anxiety, also impair sleep.
- Undiagnosed conditions like seizures, sleep apnea, or restless leg syndrome could be culprits.
- Lack of daytime exercise fails to prime the body for sleep onset at night.

Given the varied potential causes, it is important parents partner with their pediatrician to uncover and address any underlying issues sabotaging sleep. Keeping sleep logs noting bedtime, wake time, night wakings and daytime problems helps identify patterns that point to certain solutions.

Improving Bedtime Routines

Establishing a consistent, peaceful bedtime routine is essential to signal the brain and body to start winding down for rest. Core strategies include:

- Fix a set bedtime and wake time 7 days a week. Children do best with earlier bedtimes, shifting slightly later as teens.

- Design a predictable sequence of quiet evening activities to transition toward sleep. Bath, brushing teeth, pajamas, reading and relaxation techniques work well.

- Create visual schedules depicting the routine in sequence. Review each step during the day to prepare them.

- Eliminate electronics use an hour before bed as the blue light and mental stimulation inhibit natural melatonin release and drowsiness.

- Avoid high energy play, heavy meals, caffeinated foods/drinks or stressful discussions before bedtime.

- Set up a cozy sleep environment - darkened, quiet room with heavy curtains, white noise machine, weighted blanket, and comfortable mattress and bedding.

- Help them decompress before bed by providing time to discuss any worries, frustrations or emotions weighing on them.

- Try calming sensory activities before bed like full body compression rolls, gentle joint compressions, or rhythmic rocking.

- Massage and guided relaxation scripts can help ease the transition to sleep. Teach deep breathing, visualization and muscle relaxation techniques.

Consistency with these sleep hygiene steps can gradually improve the brain's cueing and expectancy around bedtime. However, it often takes weeks or months to undo years of established unhelpful sleep associations so patience is needed.

Handling Sleep Issues

When night wakings or early risers disrupt rest, parents can implement these strategies:

- Attend quickly to understand what they need - bathroom, thirst, pain, nightmare? Offer reassuring comfort.
- Keep lighting dim, voices low and interactions brief during any night interventions to signal continued sleep time.
- Remind it's still time for sleeping. Use a social story if needed to explain night versus day behaviors.
- Discourage getting fully out of bed or coming into parents' room, which strengthens undesired associations.
- Allow use of the bathroom then gently escort back to bed with verbal reminder to close eyes. Do not engage in lengthy conversations.
- For early risers, ensure the bedroom is very dark using blackout curtains. Provide calming, low stimulation activities they can do in bed until normal wake time.

- If night terrors or sleepwalking occur, gently guide them back to bed without fully waking. Ensure safety precautions like closed doors and window locks are in place.

Sometimes consistently reinforcing healthier sleep associations resolves issues. If not, discuss additional options with your pediatrician like:

- Prescription medications to help induce drowsiness and consolidate sleep cycles. These may be used short term while establishing routines.
- Bloodwork to check for nutritional deficiencies like low iron or vitamin D that could disrupt sleep.
- Referral for a sleep study to uncover issues like sleep apnea, restless leg syndrome or seizure activity during sleep.
- Metabolic testing related to melatonin production abnormalities. Melatonin supplements often help.
- Referral to a behavioral sleep specialist for customized cognitive behavioral therapy to improve sleep habits.

Teaching Sleep Self-Regulation Skills

Equipping children with relaxation and self-soothing skills helps them learn to unwind independently at night and fall back to sleep upon waking. Useful strategies to build these capabilities include:

- Create a bedtime self-regulation toolkit they can access at night - stuffed animal, soft music, favorite books, night light, journal, sensory fidgets, white noise machine, etc.
- Teach personalized relaxation skills like deep breathing, progressive muscle relaxation, and visualization they can use in bed.
- Practice meditation and mindfulness activities focused on bringing calm awareness to the present moment while lowering stress and distractions.
- Provide heavy blankets, full body compression rolls, stretches or joint compressions to incorporate deep pressure sensory input.
- Share stories modeling how characters cope with nighttime anxiety or bad dreams in healthy ways.
- Role play what to think and do upon waking at night - use bathroom, sip water, use toolkit items, and give self-instructions to relax and return to sleep. Offer rewards for returning to sleep.
- Keep cues like wake time set regardless of how early they may arise some mornings to encourage waiting calmly rather than escalating anxiety.

Building a sense of control and confidence in their ability to self-settle at night reduces distressed behaviors and motivates practicing calming strategies. Over time and with consistency, healthy sleep habits can become ingrained.

Daytime Support

Adequate nighttime sleep sets the stage for better regulated behavior during the day. Additional strategies include:

- Prioritize an exercise routine each day to prime sleep drive. Especially beneficial earlier in the day.
- Limit naps to 30 minutes, before 3pm.
- Expose them to bright natural light in the mornings to help set circadian rhythms.
- Address behavior problems possibly tied to underlying poor sleep. Adjust schedule, reduce stimulation, or teach coping skills.
- Notice and provide positive attention to desired daytime behaviors. Link acting calmly to getting enough rest.

By comprehensively addressing sleep challenges, you help ensure your child wakes each day feeling refreshed and ready to learn and engage in a positive way. Sleep is the bedrock for health, brain development and quality of life.

Chapter 8

Optimizing Your Home Environment

A safe, comfortable and structured home environment provides stability and supports the needs of children with autism. As they spend significant time in the home, assessing and optimizing factors like physical layout, sensory influences, organization and exposures is important. One key concern is mold growth, which can exacerbate autism symptoms and health challenges. This chapter will cover creating an autism-friendly home, testing for and addressing indoor mold, and additional considerations like ventilation, chemicals and lighting to enhance your living space.

Structuring a Supportive Home Environment

Aspects to evaluate when structuring your home for a child with autism include:

Physical Layout

- Define room purposes visually using colors, signs or decor. Label areas for eating, sleeping, learning, play and relaxation.
- Arrange furnishings and play/work areas to delineate activity zones and walkways. Minimize clutter tripping hazards.
- Ensure adequate storage using bins, baskets and shelving to maintain organization of environments and materials.

- Select simple, sturdy furnishings that are water/stain-resistant, comfortable and allow flexible arrangements.

- Display visual daily schedules with pictures/icons and reference calendars to provide clarity on activities and transitions.

Sensory Influences

- Reduce auditory distractions and echo by using rugs, curtains and hanging panels to soften sound transmission.

- Install dimmer switches to control bright lighting that may be visually overstimulating or irritating. Use soft, indirect lamp lighting.

- Select cooler toned soft colors for paints and decor to create calming surroundings. Avoid over-stimulating textures and excessive decorative items.

- Maintain comfortable cool temperatures and air circulation. Use a portable HEPA air filter to reduce allergens/dust.

- Provide suitable sensory materials like textured pillows, fidget toys, weighted blankets, rocking chair and exercise outlets.

- Designate a quiet space children can retreat to when emotionally or sensorily overwhelmed and comfortably decompress. Offer seating, soft lighting and tools to self-soothe.

Organization Strategies

- Maintain consistent routines for daily activities like meals, homework, chores and bedtime. Post visual schedules.

- Set designated places to sort and store items after use like backpacks, shoes, toys to promote responsibility.

- Use labeled bins, baskets and shelving to organize toys and school/art/craft supplies in a structured way accessible to the child.

- Post written or visual reminders of house rules, schedules and behavior expectations to reinforce. Review regularly.
- Limit decorative clutter and unnecessary toys. Simplify to help maintain focus. Store out of rotation toys to refresh.
- Check safety like window and door locks, electrical covers, kitchen/bath safety measures and cleaning supplies security.

Consistency, order and visual/sensory considerations tailored to your child let them feel at ease. Seek occupational therapy guidance on ideal home adaptations.

Risks and Signs of Indoor Mold

In addition to optimizing physical and sensory factors, it is vital to address any water damage, humidity and mold issues that commonly plague indoor environments. Mold growth poses particular concerns for children with autism.

Why Mold Impacts Autistic Kids

Several reasons increase susceptibility:

- Weakened immune systems - Chronic inflammation and heightened immune reactivity are common. Mold is an added exposure burden.

- Respiratory vulnerabilities - Asthma rates are higher, amplifying breathing reactions to mold.

- Sensory sensitivities - Heightened reactions to smells and chemicals make mold VOCs and mustiness intolerable.

- Habit perseveration and noticeability - Resistance to change makes remediating home environment very difficult. Mold odors prompt sensory overload.

- Behavior and sleep disturbances - Environmental mold toxins and spores exacerbate neurological symptoms, mood, focus and sleep issues.

- Hypersensitivity and absorption - Some studies note those with autism react more severely and absorb mycotoxins at higher rates, though research is limited thus far.

Due to these vulnerabilities, a mold-free living space is ideal. Let's explore common sources.

Where Mold Grows

Mold spores are present everywhere outdoors and some indoor mold spores are normal. But moisture allows rapid mold growth that leads to far higher, harmful levels that trigger reactions. Primary problem areas include:

- Flooding damage - Wet carpets, baseboards, furniture and drywall promote mold. Water from broken pipes, leaks and weather catastrophes often goes unnoticed behind walls and under materials.

- Humidity - Consistently elevated indoor humidity above 55% encourages mold growth in hidden cavities. Humid climates contribute.
- HVAC systems – Standing moisture in air ducts, coils, filters, insulation lining and condensation pans feeds mold, dispersing spores through vents.
- Bathrooms - Tile grout, showers, ceilings and walls are prone to moisture accumulation and leakage leading to colonies behind surfaces.
- Musty basements and crawl spaces - Cool, damp conditions foster mold growth on concrete, wood structures and in stored belongings.
- Wet clothes and towels - Leaving laundry wet encourages mold. Ventilate closets.
- Plumbing leaks - Slow drips within walls or under sinks/appliances allow dampness. Pipes, joints and valves deteriorate over time.
- Roof leaks and flashing failures - Water intrusion from deteriorated or damaged shingles/flashing creates wet attic areas ideal for mold. Also check siding.
- Landscaping and gutters - Runoff directed at the base of the home foundation leads to wet interiors. Clogged gutters overflow.

Be attentive to any musty odors, peeling paint or moisture indicators which signal areas to inspect closely for concealed mold issues.

Health Effects of Toxic Mold

Inhaling airborne mold spores and mycotoxins generates concerning symptoms:

- **Respiratory** - Wheezing, difficulty breathing, nasal congestion, chronic cough, pulmonary bleeding. Particularly worrisome for asthmatics

- **Immune** – Chronic colds and infections, flu-like malaise, swollen lymph nodes signaling immune reaction. May reflect elevated mycotoxin presence.

- **Neurological** – Headaches, inability to focus and concentrate, memory issues, mood changes, tremors or numbness in limbs indicating possible neuropathy.

- **Digestive upset** – Nausea, vomiting, appetite changes and abdominal pain are commonly reported in association with mold exposures.

- **Skin irritation** – Dermatitis, hives, rashes and topical infections may manifest from skin contact or airborne mold allergens.

- **Behavioral effects** – Hyperactivity, irritability, temper tantrums, sleep disruptions and sensory overload reactions are frequently cited in children after exposure.

Mycotoxins like aflatoxin, ochratoxin A, trichothecenes, and gliotoxin found in toxic molds are documented to impair cellular energy pathways, induce DNA damage, disrupt neurotransmitters, alter brain function and compromise immunity long-term. Children react at lower exposure levels than adults.

Testing for Mold

If indoor mold growth is suspected, comprehensive testing helps locate the source(s) and extent of contamination. Reliable evaluations include:

- **Detailed home inspection** – A certified mold inspector looks for condensation, leaks, humidity issues and water stains. They use infrared cameras and moisture meters to map damp areas and take swab samples of visible growth to analyze types present under the microscope. Furnishings are examined.
- **Air sampling** – Using specialized equipment, indoor and outdoor air is tested over time for mold spore types and levels. Spore counts inside should not significantly exceed outdoor levels. Swab samples may also be taken from vents to check HVAC systems.
- **Surface sampling** – Swabs of carpeting, walls and furnishings can detect mold DNA. Harder to source hidden mold without air sampling.
- **Mycotoxin testing** – Urine or blood spot analysis by specialized labs can identify presence of mycotoxins, but reference values are still emerging and insurance coverage is limited.
- **ERMI testing** – Environmental Relative Moldiness Index analysis uses advanced DNA methodology to compare mold composition in house dust to established reference standards for 37 species. High scores

indicate atypical ratios and elevated contamination. This test is affordable and you have your results back in 5 days. Uses a swifter type cloth to collect dust and dirt from around the house.

Testing performed by accredited inspectors and industrial hygienists experienced in mold analysis helps identify the scope of contamination so informed remediation can proceed.

Mold Remediation Procedures

If testing confirms atypical mold growth, abatement by properly trained professionals is vital to reduce health risks. Intensive measures often required include:

- **Source Removal** – Fix plumbing and roof leaks. Replace water damaged drywall, carpets and furnishings. Address damp crawlspaces, basements and HVAC systems. Remove moldy clothes and belongings.
- **Specialized Cleaning** – Mold-killing detergents, anti-microbial fogging treatments and dehumidification help dry, disinfect and decontaminate interiors. Air scrubbers trap spores. Protective gear should be worn.
- **Containment** – Plastic sheeting, enclosures and airlocks may be used to isolate the moldy zone while cleaning to prevent spore dispersal. Negative air pressure helps direct spores outside. Airlocks allow access.

- **Structural Repairs** – Moldy drywall, insulation, carpets, subfloors and ventilation ducts may need replacement if damage is extensive or materials porous. Evaluate options.

- **Post Cleaning Verification** – Follow up air sampling after remediation confirms spore levels have decreased to safe standards before occupancy. Installation of air purifiers adds protection.

For smaller projects, concerned homeowners can use mold killing cleaners, protective gear and HEPA filter equipped fans. Please be careful as the chemicals used can be just as toxic for your child as the mold. Use natural ingredients like white vinegar, baking soda and others. You can find many recipes on the internet. However, extensive contamination requires hazardous materials trained professionals for health's sake.

Preventing Mold Growth

After remediating mold, maintaining a mold resistant home requires vigilance:

- Fix plumbing and roof leaks promptly before water damage grows.

- Install water sensors that trigger alarms upon leakage near washing machine, water heater and sinks.

- Use dehumidifiers, ventilate bathrooms, and avoid high humidity. Ideal indoor relative humidity is 35-45%.

- Clean condensation build up on windows and walls. Fix insulation and air flow issues.

- Route rainwater drainage from landscaping away from the foundation. Clean gutters regularly.
- Keep indoor plants limited and potted properly. Be careful of introducing mold in potting soil. Monitor for standing water under pots.
- Open closets and drapes to encourage air circulation. Use cedar blocks to repel moths. Don't overcrowd closets.
- Change HVAC filters monthly. Have ductwork cleaned periodically by professionals.
- Clean bathrooms using disinfectants. Regrout tile and address leakage promptly. Install exhaust vents.
- Avoid carpets in damp prone areas. Switch to dehumidifiers instead of humidifiers.
- Inspect for hidden roof and pipe leaks annually. Check attic and crawl spaces for any dampness.
- Test indoor humidity and know optimal range for your climate. Use moisture meters to monitor.

Remaining vigilant helps safeguard your home. Trust your senses – any unusual musty smells deserve investigation. Protecting your family's health is priority.

Additional Home Environment Considerations

Beyond mold risks, a few other key home factors to optimize include:

Indoor Air Quality

- Open windows regularly for fresh air when weather permits or use whole house ventilation systems.

- Change HVAC filters monthly. Arrange professional duct cleaning every few years.

- Limit clutter that accumulates dust and choose flooring like hardwood or tile instead of carpeting.

- Run an air purifier with HEPA and activated carbon filtration to help reduce allergens, chemicals and odors.

- Check radon levels in your home periodically. Long term exposure raises lung cancer risks. Install mitigation systems if elevated.

- Avoid smoking indoors and campfire or grill smoke entering the house. Limit candles and incense.

Chemical Exposures

- Use natural cleaners like vinegar, borax and tea tree oil instead of harsh chemicals loaded with VOCs that trigger reactions. Open windows when cleaning.

- Remove shoes at the door to avoid tracking in chemicals from yard pesticides and roadway pollution.

- Choose fragrance-free laundry detergents and body care products. Fragrances contain hundreds of sensitizing chemicals.

- Ventilate the garage to prevent car exhaust and gasoline fumes from migrating indoors.

- Select solid wood furniture to avoid off-gassing of glues and chemicals from composites like pressboard. Or allow such pieces to off-gas outdoors before bringing inside.

- Test old homes for lead paint risks. Don't scrape or sand without proper abatement procedures.

Lighting Choices

Since lighting sensitivities are common with autism, install flexible lighting:

- Use dimmer switches on all overhead lights to adjust brightness as needed. Monitor for flicker which can be disruptive.

- Select bulb lighting over fluorescent which has flicker and may aggravate sensory issues.

- Look for bulbs labeled "warm color" or amber which are softer. Avoid cool blue-toned lighting.

- Place lamps in reading areas to direct light where needed without overhead glare.

- Install blackout curtains in bedrooms for darkness and regulate morning light.

- Use night lights and wall-mounted lighting along hallways for safety vs overhead lights left on.

- Teach kids to turn lights on/off themselves as desired based on their needs and comfort.

By assessing and optimizing factors from mold risks to lighting, indoor air quality, organization and layout, you can transform your home into a relaxing haven tailored to support your child's needs. Your home offers shelter in every sense of the word.

Chapter 9

Supporting Healthy Eating Habits in Autistic Children

Restrictive food preferences, limited food varieties and highly ritualized mealtime behaviors are very common among autistic children. Sensory sensitivities, rigidity around routines, oral-motor difficulties and medical issues often contribute to selective eating or nutritionally inadequate diets. With compassion, patience and creativity, parents can support expanding their child's food acceptance.

Common Dietary Patterns

Parents frequently observe eating behaviors like:

- **Food selectivity** – Only accepting a very narrow range of "safe" foods, often 5 items or less. Highly resistant to trying new foods outside preferred items. Commonly seen with kid favorites like chicken nuggets, fries, pizza, cereal, crackers.

- **Texture and consistency issues** – Only tolerating smooth, crunchy or pureed foods. Gagging or tantrums when served mixed textures orfirm foods like meats, raw veggies/fruits. Disliking "lumps."

- **Sameness in presentation** – Wanting foods prepared the exact same way every time. Distress if an item is unavailable, served on a different plate, cut differently, or brand changes.

- **Rituals around eating habits** – Needing certain utensils, seating arrangements, order of eating favorite foods first. Following rigid stepwise procedures.
- **Unusual exploratory play** – Smelling, licking, squishing, dissecting or pocketing food without eating it. Examining from all angles. Mixing different food items together.
- **Pica behavior** – Mouthing, chewing or swallowing non-edible items like paper, dirt, chalk, crayons, hair. Poses choking risks. Can indicate nutrient deficiency.
- **Oral sensitivities** – Disliking food or utensils touching mouth or lips. Gagging from metal silverware. Resists use of cups, straws or face wiping.
- **Difficulty managing utensils** – Messy grasping of spoons, trouble scooping and guiding food to mouth. Gagging on certain textures. May use hands instead.
- **Open mouth chewing** – Difficulty coordinating chewing or keeping lips closed while eating. Food may fall out of mouth.

These patterns frequently co-occur and are driven by interplay between sensory aversions, behavioral rigidity around routines, oral-motor difficulties, and medical issues like reflux or constipation. Evaluating root causes guides tactics for expanding dietary variety.

Supplementing Nutrition

When severely selective eating or oral-motor deficits exist, focus first on ensuring nutritional needs are adequately met through:

- Offering nutritious smoothies or shakes made with ingredients like Greek yogurt, avocado, nut butters, coconut milk, protein powder, spinach, berries. Provides balanced nutrition.
- Fortifying commonly accepted foods like pasta, pizza, chicken nuggets by adding in healthy fats like olive oil, ground flax, cream cheese, melted cheese and extra proteins.
- Providing nutritionally complete meal replacement drinks between meals. Watch sugar content. Higher fat and protein varieties help maintain weight.
- Pureeing or juicing fruits and vegetables into sauces and dips. Blend into soups, smoothies and baked goods.
- Choosing chewable vitamins without added sugar. Probiotic gummies support digestive health. Discuss a basic multivitamin with your pediatrician.
- Requesting blood work to check levels of iron, zinc, vitamin D, B vitamins, calcium and protein nutrition. Deficits may require supplementation.

Registering with a nutritionist or feeding therapist knowledgeable about autism is advisable to develop balanced meal plans accounting for your child's limited dietary range and sensory issues. They can recommend substituting or fortifying foods to optimize nutritional intake.

Expanding Food Acceptance

While forcing, bribing or catering typically fail to expand food repertoires long-term, repeated positive exposure in a low-pressure way can be effective. Strategies include:

- Offer new foods alongside preferred familiar items initially. Mix tiny portions of veggies into mashed potatoes or rice.
- Let them help prepare foods they are wary of trying. Grocery shopping together and engaging in meal prep promotes investment.
- Minimize texture issues by roasting, baking or grating firmer fruits and veggies rather than boiling. Offer dips like yogurt, cheese sauce or guacamole. Cut foods into tiny pieces.
- Introduce one new food at a time. Start with naturally bland, soft choices like bananas, plain pasta, or well-cooked rice. Vary cooking methods and presentation.
- Model enjoying a variety of foods at family meals. Kids are influenced by seeing others' eating habits. Never force but be an example.
- Allow casual sensory play and exploration of new foods outside of mealtimes free of eating pressure. Anything that reduces fear helps.

- Offer enthusiastic praise and non-food rewards for tolerating a new item - touching it, kissing it, licking or tasting a tiny bite. Baby steps count!

- Use a stepped gradual desensitization process from having new items simply on the plate, to touching them, kissing, licking to eventually tasting.

Your unwavering patience and compassion in the face of mealtime struggles demonstrates unconditional acceptance. With creativity and support, their dietary world can continue expanding.

Seeking Professional Support

For severe dietary limitations or concerning eating patterns, discuss referrals with your pediatrician to:

- Feeding specialists to evaluate oral-motor skills around chewing, swallowing and texture tolerance. Can help shape skills through play, exercises and desensitization.

- Speech or occupational therapists to address sensory components of feeding therapy - touching, tolerating, tasting foods.

- Allergists to test for food allergies or intolerances possibly contributing toPicky eating or GI symptoms.

- Gastroenterology specialists if reflux, constipation, diarrhea or abdominal pain affect eating.

- Nutritionists or dietitians with expertise in autism spectrum disorders for meal planning guidance to maximize nutrition.
- Psychologists or feeding clinics for cases involving extreme fear or phobias around food or eating.

With unconditional support, patience and access to knowledgeable professionals, even the pickiest eaters' food horizons can gradually expand. Let mealtimes nourish their body and their soul.

Chapter 10

Dietary Approaches for Autism Gastrointestinal Health

Many children with autism suffer from gastrointestinal symptoms like abdominal pain, constipation, diarrhea, reflux, and food intolerances. The discomfort and inflammation associated with gut issues may contribute to problem behaviors as well as nutritional deficiencies. Implementing a tailored dietary regimen under medical guidance may help alleviate gastrointestinal distress and promote overall wellbeing. This chapter will discuss using low glycemic eating, eliminating common allergens like gluten and dairy, therapeutic diets like GFCF, supplements to repair gut lining integrity, and overall nutrition tips to support your child's unique needs.

Rationale for Dietary Modifications

The causes of gastrointestinal problems in autism are multifactorial and incompletely understood. Contributing factors likely include:

- **Altered gut microbiome** - Imbalance between beneficial and pathological bacteria and yeast disrupts digestion.
- **Immune dysfunction** - Chronic inflammation and autoimmunity affect the GI tract. Elevated antibodies are common.
- **Intestinal hyperpermeability** - Lining allows passage of undigested proteins, toxins and microbes that prompt immune reactions. Leaky gut syndrome.

- **Maldigestion** - Inadequate production of digestive enzymes impairs proper breakdown of nutrients.
- **Food intolerances** - Individual sensitivity to glutens, casein milk proteins, and other items triggers inflammation.
- **Carbohydrate malabsorption** - Improper digestion of sugars and starches causes gas, pain and diarrhea. Small intestinal bacterial overgrowth is one cause.
- **Mitochondrial issues** - Cellular energy deficits affect muscular contractions that move food through the bowels.
- **Medication side effects** - Antibiotics, acid blockers and psychotropics can disrupt gut ecology and motility.
- **Behavioral factors** - Limited diet variety, poor chewing, and erratic mealtimes.

Multifactorial GI issues likely involve interconnected physiological and behavioral components. Identifying and addressing contributing factors through dietary change, testing and supplements tailored to your individual child offers hope for relieving discomfort and restoring healthy gut function.

Benefits of a Low Glycemic Diet

A low glycemic eating pattern that minimizes spike-and-crash surges in blood sugar may offer benefits:

- **Stabilizes blood sugar and energy levels** - Prevents rapid rises then steep drops that negatively affect mood, focus and hyperactivity.

- **Improves satiety** - Helps control appetite and hunger which may be disrupted in some children with autism. Reduces cravings.

- **Lessens inflammation** - Decreases GI inflammation by limiting insulin spikes that drive it. Insulin also influences gut permeability.

- **Supports microbiome** - The healthy bacteria thrive on insoluble fiber from low glycemic whole foods. This balances gut flora.

- **Enhances nutrition** - Emphasizes nutrient-dense proteins, fats, vegetables and low sugar fruits.

- **Reduces future disease risk** - Lowers risks for diabetes, obesity and cardiovascular disease later in life.

- **Improves headaches** - Some children experience less headaches and migraines on a low glycemic diet.

A low glycemic eating plan is not a quick fix miracle cure, but rather a healthy lifelong eating pattern that complements other therapies. It requires commitment and diligence but can be worthwhile for some children.

Food Guidelines for Low Glycemic Eating

Focus diet on incorporating these low or medium glycemic foods:

- Non-starchy vegetables - Greens, broccoli, tomatoes, carrots, peppers, mushrooms etc. Provides bulk and nutrients.

- Lower glycemic fruits - Berries, grapefruit, peaches, plums, cherries, apples, pears. Have more fiber.

- Lean, unprocessed meats, poultry, fish, eggs, tofu

- Nuts, seeds, nut butters

- Legumes and lentils - Kidney beans, chickpeas, peas. Choose low sodium.

- Intact whole grains - Steel cut oats, brown rice, quinoa, amaranth, millet. Rich in fiber.

- High fiber, low sugar breads and cereals - with 5g+ fiber per serving. Avoid added sugars.

- Low fat yogurt and cheese - Choose unsweetened dairy.

- Healthy fats - Olive oil, coconut oil, avocados, salmon, chia seeds.

- Spices, herbs, mustards, vinegars, lemon add lots of flavor.

Minimize high glycemic foods:

- Breads, cereals, pastas made with refined grains - White versions lack fiber.

- Starchy vegetables - Potatoes, corn, winter squash. Somewhat better if eaten whole with skin on.

- Dried fruits and juices - Fiber has been removed leaving pure concentrated sugar.

- Sweetened drinks - Sodas, juice, sports drinks, chocolate milk.

- Packaged snacks - Chips, pretzels, granola bars. Check labels for added sugars.

- Sugary desserts - Cookies, cakes, ice cream, candy. Reserve for occasional treats.

- Added sugar - Syrups, table sugar, jelly. Avoid pouring onto foods/drinks.

Getting 45-65% of calories from low glycemic carbs, 20-35% from lean proteins, and the remainder from healthy fats and veggies is optimal for filling, nutritious meals. Work up gradually in increasing dietary fiber sources to allow the digestive tract time to adjust and prevent gas or bloating. Drinking enough water is essential.

Sample Low Glycemic Meal Plan

Breakfast:

- Steel cut oatmeal made with milk, topped with berries and walnuts
- Veggie omelet with avocado and cheese
- Peanut butter on sprouted whole grain toast
- Greek yogurt topped with chia seeds, apple and cinnamon

Lunch:

- Lentil vegetable soup with whole grain crackers
- Tuna salad wrap in whole wheat tortilla with carrots sticks
- Turkey and provolone sandwich on sprouted whole grain bread
- Quinoa tabbouleh salad with chickpeas and cucumbers

Dinner:

- Baked salmon over roasted Brussels sprouts and brown rice pilaf
- Turkey chili with black beans over baked sweet potato
- Chicken fajitas with peppers and onion on corn tortillas
- Pasta with turkey meatballs and marinara sauce with side salad

Snacks:

- Sliced pear with nut butter

- Cottage cheese with peach slices

- Hummus with raw veggie sticks

- Trail mix with nuts, seeds and dried cranberries

- Plain popcorn sprinkled with nutritional yeast

- Apple slices with natural almond butter

Beverages:

- Water, herbal tea, seltzer

- Low fat milk, fortified non-dairy milks

- Fresh lemon water

Being consistent about limiting refined carbohydrates and added sugars takes diligence but pays off by providing steady energy, more balanced behavior, and reducing GI symptoms. Over time, cravings fade. Work closely with your doctor and nutrition experts.

The Gluten-Free, Casein-Free Diet

For children with food intolerances, eliminating inflammatory foods is beneficial. Gluten and casein proteins found in wheat, barley, rye and dairy products are common triggers. Some parents report GI symptom relief, less brain fog, and improvements in behavior and focus when fully removing these proteins.

Potential mechanisms:

- **Leaky gut** - Partially digested glutens and casein may enter bloodstream and provoke immune reactions in those with intestinal hyperpermeability.
- **Opioid excess** - Peptides from gluten and casein can exert morphine-like effects on the brain, worsening autism symptoms.

Implementing a strict gluten-free, casein-free (GFCF) diet eliminates exposure to these problematic proteins but requires vigilance. Contamination and hidden sources are common. It necessitates preparing mostly homemade meals and carefully reading labels, as gluten and dairy byproducts are added throughout processed foods.

Potential pitfalls include inadequate nutrition, especially calcium, fiber and B vitamins. Nutritional supplements and consultation with a knowledgeable nutritionist is advised to prevent deficiencies. Some children experience difficult withdrawal initially when eliminating gluten and casein. Improvements emerge gradually over the months as inflammation subsides.

For best success, the GFCF diet must be implemented fully. Just reducing gluten or casein intake rarely provides benefit. Close medical monitoring is essential, especially for young children. Pros and cons must be weighed carefully.

Dairy-Free Considerations

Eliminating casein by going dairy-free means excluding:

- Milk, ice cream, yogurt, sour cream, cream cheese, butter, ghee
- Cheese in all forms
- Whey protein powders
- Many packaged snacks, breads, sauces, and baked goods

Provide alternate sources of calcium like leafy greens, calcium-set tofu, nuts, beans, fortified non-dairy milks and juices. Many children tolerate goat or sheep dairy better than cow. Rice milk should be avoided due to arsenic concerns. Take care to ensure adequate protein intake without dairy as a source.

Implementing the diet requires learning new recipes and careful label reading. Being milk-free necessitates substitutions like non-dairy milks, vegan butter, coconut creamer and vegan cheese. With some adjustments, it is certainly doable. Monitor nutrition and reactions closely.

Going Gluten-Free

A gluten-free diet eliminates all wheat, barley, rye and derivatives by avoiding:

- Breads, cereals, crackers, baked goods unless certified gluten-free
- Pasta, wheat flour, breadcrumbs, pancake/waffle mixes (use gluten-free versions)
- Beer, ales and lagers (most are gluten-based)
- Soy sauce and teriyaki sauces
- Many packaged soups, sauces, salad dressings and seasoned snack foods

Gluten-free whole grains like rice, corn, buckwheat, certified oats, quinoa, amaranth and millet become staples instead. Be aware that "wheat-free" doesn't equal gluten-free, as barley and rye also contain gluten proteins. It is important to read labels diligently.

Many children benefit from removing inflammatory triggers like gluten and casein. While challenging to implement strictly, a trial period of 2-3 months helps determine if GI, behavioral and cognitive issues improve significantly to make the effort worthwhile.

Lactose-Free Diet for Lactose Intolerance

Some children have lactose intolerance meaning they lack sufficient lactase enzymes to properly digest the milk sugar lactose. This is distinct from a milk protein allergy to casein. Going lactose-free eliminates dairy products containing lactose:

- Milk, ice cream, yogurt, puddings, cream
- Soft cheeses like ricotta, cottage, cream cheese
- Prepackaged foods with milk additives

Lactose-free milk, hard aged cheeses like cheddar and Swiss, and yogurt with active cultures are usually well tolerated even with lactose intolerance. Various non-dairy milks and ice creams made from soy, almond, coconut, rice or oats can be substitutes. Oral lactase enzyme tablets which provide missing enzymes may allow some dairy consumption.

Common symptoms of lactose intolerance are gas, diarrhea, cramping and nausea after consuming dairy products. Breath testing and reducing lactose for 1-2 weeks under a doctor's supervision can confirm if lactose intolerance exists and requires dietary restriction.

Additional Dietary Approaches

Specialized diets like the Specific Carbohydrate Diet, Anti-Candida Diet, and GAPS Diet are sometimes used for autism gastrointestinal issues. They can be highly restrictive and difficult to implement fully, especially for picky eaters. Progress requires strict adherence. The risk of nutritional shortfalls is higher with extreme limitations. Professional medical guidance Monitoring is mandatory. Research on efficacy is limited.

Common questions about popular diets:

Specific Carbohydrate Diet (SCD) – Removes all grains, starches, sugars, processed foods, most dairy. Allow monosaccharides. Focuses on homemade 24-hour fermented yogurt from goat or camel milk, meat, nuts, certain fruits and non-starchy vegetables. Expensive and not meal-friendly.

Anti-Candida Diet – Eliminates sugar, gluten, dairy, fruit, starchy vegetables to discourage yeast overgrowth. Very restrictive. Die-off reactions can occur when yeast rapidly releases toxins. Challenging to maintain long-term.

Elimination Diet - Removes potential trigger foods like gluten, dairy, soy, nuts, eggs one at a time to identify intolerances. Reintroduction to confirm. Helps personalize diet. The risk of inadequate nutrition if overly limited.

GAPS Diet - Uses food stages to "seal" the gut lining. Later systematically reintroduces foods. Relies heavily on bone broths, fermented foods and high-fat meats and yogurt. Very intense and time-consuming. Efficacy is still under investigation.

Paleo Diet - Focuses on foods presumed eaten in the Paleolithic era - lean meats, fish, vegetables, nuts, seeds, oils. Excludes dairy, grains, legumes, processed foods and sugar. May reduce inflammation. Higher protein needs planning to avoid excess.

Low FODMAP - Reduces indigestible carbs called FODMAPs (fermentable oligosaccharides, disaccharides, monosaccharides and polyols) found in certain fruits, grains, vegetables and dairy that can trigger IBS symptoms like gas, cramping and diarrhea in those sensitive. Complicated to implement properly. Needs guidance.

No one universally ideal diet exists given the heterogeneity of autism. An elimination trial may pinpoint problematic foods. However, over restriction poses risks for nutritional shortfalls in growing children. Work closely with your doctor to weigh pros and cons. Focus on identifying and providing the foods your individual child tolerates and requires for balanced nutrition.

Gut-Supporting Supplements

Discuss adding the following supplements tailored to your child's needs with your physician to improve gastrointestinal health:

- Probiotics support healthy gut flora. Broad spectrum brands with diverse bacterial strains are best. Reduce constipation, diarrhea and inflammation.
- Digestive enzymes taken with meals improve breakdown of proteins, carbs and fats, reducing pain and bloating.
- Omega-3 fatty acids are anti-inflammatory and maintain gut barrier integrity. Fish oil capsules or algae-derived DHA are options.
- Glutamine powder promotes healing of intestinal cell lining and reduces permeability. Doses of 10-30 g daily in divided amounts.
- Quercetin has antioxidant and anti-inflammatory properties that help stabilize mast cells and reduce immune reactions. 100-500 mg daily.
- Zinc supports immune function and production of stomach acid. Limit to 30 mg daily.
- Vitamin D influences gut immunity. Optimal levels around 50 ng/ml. Supplement if low.

Improving gastrointestinal health through dietary changes, probiotics, gut-supportive nutrients tailored to your child's needs and doctor-monitored elimination diets may relieve chronic symptoms. Always focus on optimal nutrition as the priority.

Nutrition Tips for Autistic Children

Alongside therapeutic diets or restrictions, parents can support their child's nutritional health by:

- Choosing organic when possible to reduce pesticide residues. Peel conventionally grown produce.
- Preparing healthy grab-and-go snacks like turkey wraps, smoothies and cut veggie packs for busy days.
- Trying different cooking methods - roast, stir fry, blend into baked goods and smoothies. Cut foods into fun shapes.
- Being creative to increase nutrients - add chia, spinach, nut butters into waffles, muffins, yogurt and smoothies.
- Allowing relaxed grazing of snacks versus structured meals if sitting still is difficult.
- Focusing on finding at least one food from each category they accept. Build from there.
- Reading labels for hidden ingredients like milk solids, sugar, wheat starch etc. Call manufacturers to inquire.
- Discussing customized vitamin/mineral supplements to fill any nutritional gaps identified through testing.
- Watching portion sizes if overweight. Limiting high calorie extras and snacks helps balance intake.
- Involving your child in preparing and choosing healthy foods when possible. They're more likely to sample what they help make.

By working closely with medical and nutritional experts who understand your child's physiology, dietary changes can be implemented carefully with the goal of reducing gastrointestinal and behavioral symptoms through optimizing gut health and nutrition. Stay the course - it can take months of consistency to determine efficacy of an approach. Focus on nourishing the body and the soul.

Chapter 11

Nutritional and Natural Supplements for Autism Support

Along with behavioral interventions and therapies, parents and clinicians have turned to natural supplements and vitamins as complementary medicine alternatives for addressing some of the physiological factors associated with autism spectrum disorder (ASD). While not cure-alls, certain vitamins, minerals, probiotics, enzymes and other natural agents show promise in helping improve gastrointestinal health, immune regulation, neurological function and symptoms like anxiety, focus and behavioral control when incorporated into a comprehensive treatment plan. Always consult with your child's doctor before starting any new supplement, natural product or dietary regimen.

Probiotics

Probiotics are beneficial strains of live bacteria and yeast that help populate our digestive tracts and mucosa and modulate the gut microbiome. Common probiotic species include Lactobacilli, Bifidobacteria, Saccharomyces and others. Emerging research indicates gut flora may influence brain health and behavior through the gut-brain axis as microbial metabolites cross the blood-brain barrier.

Children with ASD frequently have altered gut ecology with less microbial diversity, fewer beneficial bacteria and overgrowth of potentially pathogenic strains. Probiotics aim to rebalance this ecosystem. Potential benefits include:

- Alleviate gastrointestinal issues like constipation, diarrhea, abdominal discomfort, gut permeability.
- Reduce pro-inflammatory cytokines and promote healthy immune regulation.
- Improve nutritional status by supporting digestion and absorption.
- Produce positive metabolites and neurotransmitters like GABA that influence brain function and mental health.
- Protect against opportunistic infections like Candida yeast overgrowths.
- Support healthier expression of genetic material through beneficial epigenetic effects

Look for broad spectrum probiotic supplements with diverse strains, at least 10 billion CFUs, and verified viability through expiration. Can be taken as capsules or powders. Start low and gradually increase to avoid initial gas or bloating. Pair with prebiotics like inulin, FOS or arabinogalactans to nourish probiotic growth.

Omega-3 Fatty Acids

Omega-3s like EPA and DHA found abundantly in fatty fish are essential fatty acids with robust anti-inflammatory, brain supporting and cardiovascular benefits. They are crucial for healthy prenatal and childhood development. Children with ASD often have inadequate intake from diet and display altered fatty acid metabolism.

Omega-3s dampen inflammation, boost learning and cognition, improve focus and behavior, and may benefit:

- Cognitive skills and language development when mothers supplement during pregnancy and infancy
- Hyperactivity, impulsivity, tantrums, irritability and self-injury
- Sleep quality and duration
- Anxiety, OCD and depressive symptoms
- Gastrointestinal inflammation and motility
- Skin conditions like eczema and allergies
- Heart health and triglycerides later in life
- Joint pain and muscular aches
- Immunity and autoimmune regulation

Aim for 1-1.5 grams daily of combined EPA/DHA. Fish oil, cod liver oil, krill oil or algae-based supplements boost intake levels. Pair with vitamin E to prevent oxidation. Check for purity.

Digestive Enzymes

Many children with ASD have reduced digestive secretions of enzymes like proteases, lipases and disaccharidases needed to properly break down proteins, fats, carbohydrates, dairy and gluten. This prevents proper nutrient absorption. Contributing factors may include:

- Pancreatic insufficiency - inadequate enzyme output
- Decreased gut motility - slow transit time reduces exposure to enzymes
- Gastric acid inhibition - antacids and acid reducing medications impair digestion
- Inflammation and infection - impairs digestive processes

Digestive enzymes taken with meals or snacks can improve breakdown and absorption of nutrients, lessening gastrointestinal discomfort, bloating, gas and diarrhea. Key enzymes to look for:

- Proteases - break down protein chains into amino acids
- Lipases - split dietary fats into absorbable fatty acids and glycerides
- Amylases - cleave carbohydrate molecules into simple sugars
- Lactase - needed by those deficient in breaking down lactose in dairy
- Peptidases - break down peptides and ease issues with gluten/casein
- Alpha-galactosidase - helps metabolize certain carbohydrates

Enzymes with main meals minimizes digestion taxing the gastrointestinal system and optimizes nutritional status. Aim for full spectrum blends.

Here is a section on the benefits of vitamin A supplementation that can be added to the previous chapter:

Vitamin A

Vitamin A is a fat-soluble nutrient obtained from retinol in animal foods and carotenoid precursors like beta-carotene found in plant foods. It is essential for vision, gene transcription, immune function, skin health, antioxidant activity and embryonic development.

Some studies note vitamin A deficiencies in a subset of children with autism, as well as benefits from supplementation. Potential mechanisms of action include:

- Potent antioxidant activity from scavenging free radicals and reactive oxygen species that cause oxidative stress.
- Supporting healthy vision, corneal surface, tear production and strength of eye tissues.
- Regulating gene expression during fetal development by influencing DNA transcription and expression of genetic information.
- Supporting immune competence through differentiation and proliferation of B and T cells. Enhances efficacy of vaccines.
- Nourishing respiratory health by maintaining mucus membrane integrity and cilia motility to clear airways.
- Promoting skin integrity and wound healing. Deficiency manifests in dryness and lesions.

- Supporting taste bud and sensory nerve function. Deficiency numbs sensitivity.

Work with your doctor to test levels if deficiency is suspected. Supplement oral vitamin A as retinyl palmitate or retinyl acetate. Cod liver oil also provides vitamin A. Usual doses are 5,000-25,000 IU for children depending on status. Preformed vitamin A can build up to toxic levels so professional oversight on dosing is important.

Vitamin D

Nearly a third of children on the spectrum have insufficient blood levels of the "sunshine vitamin" best obtained through sunlight, fish and supplements. Vitamin D is crucial for bone health, immunity, mood regulation, brain development and genetic expression. Deficits are linked to autism severity.

Vitamin D dampens inflammation, enhances production of serotonin and oxytocin, regulates over 200 genes, and supports:

- Bone density and preventing rickets
- Muscular and cardiovascular function
- Immune regulation and respiratory health
- Brain development and cognition
- Reduced autoimmunity and cancer risks
- Better sleep quality and duration

Have your child's 25-hydroxy vitamin D level tested. Optimal values are 50-80 ng/mL. Supplement with vitamin D3 as needed to maintain recommended range, under a doctor's guidance. Take vitamin K2 to direct calcium properly.

Zinc

Zinc is an essential mineral for growth, gastrointestinal health, immunity and neurological function. Nutrient deficits are frequently noted in those with ASD. Zinc is vital for:

- Growth and sexual maturation
- Appetite and digestion
- Skin, hair, nail and eye health
- Immune cell activity and detoxification
- Cognition, learning and sensory processing
- Gene expression and brain plasticity
- Regulation of copper and vitamin A

Zinc deficiencies can manifest in picky eating, poor growth, frequent illness, leaky gut and behavioral problems. Aim for up to 30 mg of supplemental zinc daily with food, preferably as zinc picolinate or zinc glycinate for absorption. Check copper levels, as zinc lowers copper.

Vitamin B6 with Magnesium

Vitamin B6 (pyridoxine) is a crucial co-factor for over 140 biochemical reactions related to metabolism, neurological function, immune activity and methylation. Some children with autism have trouble converting B6 to its active form. Magnesium improves activation.

Together B6 and magnesium offer benefits for:

- Hemoglobin production and circulation
- Liver detoxification and glutathione antioxidant activity
- Neurotransmitter synthesis like GABA, dopamine and serotonin
- Energy production and enzymatic reactions
- Joint flexibility, bone health and muscular movement
- Gene expression and methylation processes
- Reducing irritability, hyperactivity and self-stimulatory behaviors

Dose B6 carefully under medical guidance as high levels can become neurotoxic. Start with around 25-50 mg of B6 twice daily with the same amount of magnesium and titrate based on needs and effects. Deficiencies present risks so work with a knowledgeable practitioner.

Magnesium Oil

Transdermal magnesium chloride oil absorbed through the skin bypasses digestion to directly replenish cellular magnesium levels. Many children with ASD are deficient in this crucial mineral involved in over 300 bodily processes.

Benefits of magnesium oil include:

- Increases cellular magnesium absorption faster than oral supplements.
- Reduces magnesium deficiency at the neurological level to enhance learning, memory, cognition and behavior.
- Eases anxiety, hyperactivity, restlessness and insomnia.
- Relaxes tight and cramped muscles. Eases body aches and growing pains.
- Provides antioxidant support and stabilizes cell membranes.
- Anti-inflammatory effects on joints, tissues and nerves.
- Improves some autistic behaviors like eye contact and social interaction.

Magnesium chloride oil is applied and absorbed trans dermally after being diluted in a carrier oil like coconut oil. Start slowly and increase gradually from 1-2 sprays daily to avoid loose stools. Oral magnesium should also be supplemented. Kids often enjoy the calming massage of magnesium oil before bed.

Melatonin

Melatonin is our natural sleep-wake cycle regulating hormone produced by the pineal gland in response to darkness. Many children on the spectrum have low melatonin levels and sleep disturbances. Melatonin promotes:

- Deeper, more restorative quality sleep. Improves sleep onset.
- Circadian rhythm synchronization and morning alertness
- Muscle relaxation aiding sleep and reduced tics
- Anti-inflammatory and antioxidant support
- Immune system regulation and gastrointestinal protection
- Relief of anxiety and better mood regulation

Melatonin must be used carefully in children, as response is highly individualized. While generally considered safe, there is limited long-term safety data. Paradoxical reactions like increased energy or opposite sleep-wake cycle are possible. Start with a very low dose of 0.5-1 mg standard melatonin 30-60 minutes before bedtime and only increase gradually if desired sleep improvements do not occur. Slow release formulations are preferable. Carefully monitor the timing, dose and effects under pediatrician guidance, as smaller doses can be more effective than higher amounts. Stop if any concerning side effects develop. Melatonin should not be used in all children, especially those with seizure disorders or taking other sleep, psychiatric or immune-modulating medications.

Probiotics

Probiotics are beneficial strains of live bacteria and yeasts that populate our digestive tracts and mucosa, improving the microbial balance. Common probiotics include Lactobacillus, Bifidobacteria, certain Bacillus species and Saccharomyces strains. Research confirms children with autism frequently have altered gut flora with less diversity, fewer beneficial microbes and overgrowth of potentially pathogenic bacteria and yeast.

Probiotics aim to crowd out unhealthy flora and restore equilibrium. Potential benefits include:

- Alleviate gastrointestinal issues like constipation, diarrhea, reflux, abdominal pain
- Reduce gut epithelium permeability and pro-inflammatory cytokines
- Improve nutritional and immune status
- Produce beneficial metabolites that influence brain function and mental health
- Protect against infections and overgrowth like Candida
- Support healthier expression of genetic material through epigenetic effects

Look for broad spectrum blends with at least 10 billion CFUs per serving and guaranteed viability through expiration. Should contain diverse Lactobacillus, Bifidobacterium and other strains. Can be taken as capsules or powders. Start low and gradually increase dosage to avoid initial gas or bloating. To nourish probiotic growth, pair with prebiotic fibers like inulin, FOS and arabinogalactans.

Ashwagandha

Ashwagandha (Withania somnifera) is an adaptogenic herb used in Ayurvedic healing traditions. Its root powder contains bioactive withanolides that modulate key neurotransmitters and hormones involved in managing stress and regulating physiological processes.

For children with autism, ashwagandha may:

- Improve focus, attention span and learning capacity. Enhances memory retrieval.
- Reduce anxiety, obsessive compulsive behaviors and restlessness. Induces calmness.
- Stabilize mood and emotional reactivity. Lessens aggressive outbursts.
- Increase social interaction and communication skills. Improves eye contact.
- Boost immunity against infections through immunomodulating effects.
- Regulate thyroid hormone levels. Support healthy growth and development.
- Reduce inflammation, mitigate cellular oxidation and induce phase 2 liver detox enzymes.

Typical doses range from 125-500 mg daily of standardized extract, depending on age and weight. Should be avoided in hyperthyroidism or autoimmune conditions and used cautiously with other immune or thyroid medications. Work with an integrative pediatrician on appropriate use. Effects may take 2-3 weeks to manifest.

Broccoli Seed Extract

Broccoli and other cruciferous vegetables contain a compound called sulforaphane that exhibits antioxidant, anti-inflammatory, and detoxification-enhancing effects. Broccoli seed extract and broccoli sprout powder concentrates provide a more potent source of sulforaphane.

As an inducer of the body's natural detoxification enzymes, sulforaphane may help children with autism by:

- Activating the Nrf2 pathway that enhances production of glutathione, superoxide dismutase and other protective antioxidants.
- Improving efficiency of Phase 1 and Phase II liver detoxification enzymes to bind and eliminate heavy metals like mercury.
- Reducing neuroinflammation through inhibition of pro-inflammatory cytokines, NF-kB and COX enzymes.
- Protecting mitochondria, the cellular energy factories, from oxidative damage.

- Increasing levels of beneficial gut bacteria like Lactobacilli and Bifidobacteria species.

- Providing high levels of other beneficial phytochemicals found in cruciferous vegetables.

Broccoli seed extract contains the highest percentage of precursor glucoraphanin which converts to active sulforaphane. Typical doses range from 25-200 mg daily. It has an excellent safety profile, though those taking blood thinners or medications should discuss with a doctor first.

Curcumin

Curcumin is the bioactive compound that gives turmeric spice its vibrant golden hue and potent medicinal properties. It provides strong anti-inflammatory, antioxidant, antiviral, antibacterial and anticancer effects with multiple health applications. For autism, curcumin may:

- Dampen chronic inflammation and mast cell activation

- Quell gastrointestinal distress and normalize intestinal permeability

- Stimulate growth of Akkermansia muciniphila involved in formation of gut barrier protective mucus

- Reduce oxidative stress and free radical damage

- Support healthy liver detoxification and glutathione production

- Influence gene expression through epigenetic effects

- Boost blood-brain barrier integrity to exclude toxins and pathogens

- Modulate key signaling pathways and neurotransmitters involved in mood, cognition and behavior
- Increase brain derived neurotrophic factor BDNF needed for healthy neurodevelopment

Look for enhanced bioavailable forms like curcumin phytosomes. Pair with black pepper for further absorption. Start low at 50 mg daily and increase slowly to 200-500 mg twice daily with food. Watch for gastric side effects. Avoid in gallstones or bile duct issues.

Methylfolate and Methyl-B12

Folates (folic acid or vitamin B9) and cobalamin (B12) play interconnected roles in cellular energy, methylation chemistry, neurotransmitter synthesis, DNA/RNA formation and managing oxidative stress through homocysteine reduction. Methylfolate and methylcobalamin are the bioactive forms, which some children have difficulty converting from regular folic acid and cyanocobalamin.

Together, bioavailable methylfolate and methyl-B12 enhance:

- Nucleic acid synthesis and stability of DNA and RNA
- Nerve conduction, myelination of neurons and neurotransmitter production
- One-carbon methylation cycle reactions and gene expression

- Detoxification, antioxidant status and reduction of hyperhomocysteinemia

- Cholesterol metabolism, vascular and heart health

- Red and white blood cell formation and leukocyte function

- Energy production and stabilization of cell membranes

Dosing of methylfolate and methyl-B12 used individually or in combination supplements like CerefolinNAC should be overseen by a knowledgeable physician, but typically ranges from 400-2000 mcg (0.4-2 mg) based on lab testing and clinical presentation. Deficiencies manifest in neurological symptoms. Use activated forms.

Saccharomyces boulardii

Saccharomyces boulardii is a tropical strain of yeast that exerts multiple health benefits, especially for digestive support. As a probiotic, its unique mechanisms include:

- Reducing pro-inflammatory cytokines and mast cell activation

- Increasing production of secretory IgA immune defenses

- Blocking adhesion and binding of unhealthy bacteria and Candida to intestinal lining

- Neutralizing certain bacterial toxins and reducing virulence

- Restoring healthy intestinal permeability and gut motility

S. boulardii is beneficial for:

- Alleviating gastrointestinal distress like diarrhea, constipation and IBS
- Improving microbial balance by crowding out Candida overgrowth
- Aiding digestion and restoration of normal GI function
- Boosting immunity and reducing gut inflammatory response
- Helping resolve Clostridioides difficile infection

Typical dosing ranges from 250-750 mg daily taken apart from food and antibiotics which can destroy S. Boulardii. It generally has an excellent safety profile. Avoid in immunosuppression or fungal allergy.

Acetyl-L-Carnitine

Acetyl-L-carnitine (ALCAR) is an amino acid derivative of L-carnitine that crosses the blood-brain barrier to support energy metabolism and neurological function. It provides bioavailable acetic acid and aids transport of fatty acids into mitochondria for energy production.

ALCAR may benefit children with ASD by:

- Improving mitochondrial function and cellular energy efficiency. Counteracts oxidative stress.
- Supporting production of key neurotransmitters like acetylcholine and GABA.

- Enhancing learning capacity, cognition, memory formation and recall.
- Reducing hyperactivity and impulsivity while improving motivation and attention.
- Lessening repetitive behaviors and obsessive-compulsive tendencies.
- Improving social cognition, emotional recognition and regulation.

Typical supplemental doses of ALCAR range from 200-500 mg once or twice daily for children based on age, weight and sensitivity screening under medical guidance. It has low toxicity but high doses may cause overstimulation or hypomania. Effects are gradual over 2-3 months.

L-Carnosine

Carnosine is a naturally occurring antioxidant dipeptide composed of beta-alanine and histidine amino acids. It is found abundantly in skeletal muscle and in lesser amounts in nervous tissue. As an intracellular buffer, carnosine stabilizes cell membranes and pH, shielding tissues from oxidative stress. It has neuroprotective effects.

Carnosine benefits autism by:

- Scavenging damaging reactive oxygen species and free radicals
- Chelating heavy metals to promote excretion and reduce toxicity

- Suppressing formation of advanced glycation end-products that trigger inflammation
- Supporting healthy cellular respiration and energy metabolism
- Calming activated microglia immune cells and suppressing excess inflammation
- Potentially enhancing frontal lobe function and cognition
- Improving muscle contraction and physical endurance capacity

Typical dosing is around 800-2000 mg daily divided for children, either using L-carnosine capsules or patented L-carnosine compounds like CarnoSyn. It has a high safety profile. Those with shellfish allergy should avoid.

Selected Botanicals and Extracts

Certain plant-derived extracts offer therapeutic effects for autism symptoms:

Bacopa monnieri – Ayurvedic nootropic that enhances cognition, memory and attention. Antioxidant adaptogen that lowers anxiety and stress. Dose 100-400 mg daily.

Lemon balm – Anxiolytic GABA-stimulating herb to reduce anxiety and promotes calmness. Mildly antiviral and antibacterial also. Dose 300-600 mg daily.

French maritime pine bark extract – Potent antioxidant that improves circulation, reduces inflammation, protects neurons and enhances cognition. Dose 50-200 mg daily.

Passionflower – Herbal anxiolytic that increases GABA activity and alpha brain waves to lessen anxious thoughts and enhance relaxation. Dose 90-360 mg daily.

Valerian root – Sedative effects to relieve sleep problems and anxiety. Increases GABA while lowering glutamate. Typical doses of 150-450 mg.

Always consult licensed healthcare practitioners like naturopaths before initiating botanical protocols, especially with very young children or complex cases. Many other specialized extracts like ashwagandha, rhodiola rosea, ginseng, St. John's wort and saffron may also be beneficial.

Gastrointestinal and Digestive Support Options

GI complications are very prevalent in ASD. A variety of natural remedies help heal and protect the gut lining, reduce inflammation, improve digestion, microbial balance and symptom relief.

Digestive Enzymes – Oral proteases, lipases and disaccharidases improve digestion of proteins, fats and carbohydrates for better nutrient absorption and reduced abdominal discomfort.

Demulcent Herbs – Marshmallow, slippery elm and licorice root coat and soothe intestinal lining and reduce hypersensitivity reactions. Useful for reflux, constipation or diarrhea.

DGL – Deglycyrrhizinated licorice without glycyrrhizin is gentler on the stomach for chronic gastritis and GERD. Increases protective mucus. 75-900 mg chewed before meals.

Aloe Vera Gel – Soothes irritated digestive tract, stomach ulcers and reflux. Reduces gut inflammatory cytokines. 2-4 ounces pure juice daily.

Slippery elm – Demulcent that forms gelatinous fiber to relieve gut irritation. Also helps constipation. 1 tsp or 200 mg capsules.

Marshmallow root – Demulcent herb traditionally used for soothing coughs, ulcers and urinary irritation. Helps protect and heal irritated GI tract mucosa when inflammation, infection or ulceration present.

Ginger – Carminative that reduces gas, bloating, diarrhea and abdominal cramping due to potent anti-inflammatory compounds called gingerols. Dose 0.5-2 grams powdered.

Peppermint Oil – Alleviates IBS symptoms like abdominal pain and bloating via smooth muscle relaxation. Also reduces headache pain. Enteric coated is best. 0.2-0.4 ml capsules.

Artichoke Leaf – Stimulates bile flow to aid digestion and gut motility. Helpful for indigestion, dyspepsia and functional GI issues like IBS. Standardized extract 150-1200 mg daily.

Fiber Supplements – Psyllium, acacia fiber, partially hydrolyzed guar gum ease constipation by increasing stool bulk and moisture. Start low and build up.

Rice Bran Fiber – High insoluble fiber without gluten for regularity. 10-30 grams daily. Also contains B vitamins and protease enzymes.

Other specialized compounds like L-glutamine powder, NAC, triphala, quercetin and oil of oregano can also support gut healing and restoration under supervision. A healthy GI tract lays the foundation for overall wellbeing.

Chapter 12

Supporting Your Child in School

Ensuring your child has the tools and supports to fully participate and thrive academically, socially and behaviorally at school is a key priority for parents. Being actively involved, educating staff, utilizing special education services, and selecting optimal educational settings are crucial to promoting progress. With collaboration and advocacy, you can help create an environment where your child can flourish.

Building Collaboration with Your Child's School

Frequent communication creates partnership between home and school, setting students up for success:

- Share observations from home on your child's skills, interests, learning preferences, motivators, triggers and approaches that work well or cause frustration.
- Offer insights on how your child communicates, follows instructions, processes information, handles transitions and manages frustration. Help teachers "see through their eyes."
- Ask how your child interacts with peers, navigates the daily classroom routine, follows rules and meets academic expectations. Check on any problem behaviors.

- Request consistent home-school communication through notebooks, emails, phone calls or meetings to discuss progress, concerns, goals and strategies.
- Attend parent-teacher conferences, IEP meetings and other check-ins. Come prepared with goals and questions. Politely advocate for needed supports.
- Volunteer, have lunch at school or observe classes when possible to get a firsthand view. This helps inform accommodation requests.
- Provide positive feedback when teachers make efforts to connect with your child, tailor teaching strategies to their learning needs, and support positive behavior. Feeling genuinely valued motivates staff.

By proactively sharing knowledge of your child and collaborating in decision-making, staff can better customize teaching methods, expectations and behavior plans. Maintain contact and speak up any time your child's needs aren't being adequately addressed.

Educating School Staff

Don't assume staff automatically have adequate understanding of autism spectrum disorders or your individual child's needs. Kindly offer resources and guidance:

- Share articles and fact sheets explaining autism characteristics like sensory sensitivity, social skills gaps, communication challenges, need for routines and how these affect learning.

- Explain how autism manifests specifically in your child - what motivates them, triggers distress, calms them, preferred learning styles. Help personalize autism.

- Provide recommendations on evidence-based classroom supports like visual schedules, warnings before transitions, fidgets, headphones and opportunities for movement breaks.

- Offer to provide training or bring in experts to teach staff best ways to reinforce positive behavior, prevent sensory overload, and safely deescalate meltdowns. Many want to help but simply don't know how.

- Correct terminology, language or stereotypes that generalize, stigmatize or undermine the potential in those with autism. Model strengths-based, respectful "person first language."

- Highlight the diverse capabilities and strengths in your child. Emphasize focusing on developing talents not just remediating deficits. Share successes!

By championing your child's needs and autism awareness, you pave the way for an educational environment tailored to help them thrive academically, socially and behaviorally. Your knowledge and guidance builds staff empathy and competence.

Overview of Special Education Services

Two primary avenues exist for accessing supports and therapies through the school system:

504 Plans – Focus on accommodations and modifications to the general education program so students can fully access curriculum and activities. Used for mild to moderate disability needs. Common supports include:

- Permission to leave class as needed for sensory/emotional breaks to manage overload or anxiety.
- Adjustments to assignments like extra time on tests, shorter tasks, spacing out work and breaking into steps.
- Assistive technology provisions like tablets, read-aloud programs, audio books or laptops.
- Modified seating arrangements like front of class or quiet workstations to limit distractions.
- Explicit teaching of organizational and social skills needed to participate in classes.
- Adjusted attendance or school day schedule if needed to accommodate therapy appointments.

Individualized Education Programs (IEPs) – For students needing specialized instruction and more intensive interventions. Legally-binding documents tailored annual to each child's evolving needs:

- Measurable academic, communication, motor, social and behavioral goals targeting priority skill deficits. Goals are reviewed and updated yearly.
- Amount of time to be spent in general education classes versus special education life skills or therapy groups. Determines degree of inclusion.
- Individual therapies like occupational, physical and speech therapy provided during school hours. Social skills groups.
- Positive behavior reinforcement plan and crisis intervention plan if behaviors disrupt learning. Safety measures may be included.
- Transition planning services as they reach adulthood like vocational training, independent living skills and continued therapies or tutoring.

Having a comprehensive evaluation conducted provides eligibility for these formal services. Approval criteria, service availability and quality vary greatly by state and district, however. Availability of experienced autism professionals is especially uneven. This underscores the value of parents being informed self-advocates.

Selecting Optimal Educational Settings

Children learn and thrive in diverse environments. Consider your child's learning profile and needs when exploring settings like traditional mainstream classes with support, dedicated special education life skills/resource rooms, specialized autism cluster programs within schools, private autism-focused schools or therapy centers, online learning and homeschooling. Compare:

- How curriculum and teaching is adapted to learning styles of those with autism - visual, hands-on, concrete.
- Opportunities for peer interaction and friendship to naturally learn social rules and communication.
- Training of staff on evidence-based techniques like Applied Behavior Analysis and sensory supports. Knowledge of autism among administrators and educators.
- Consistent availability of autism specialists like speech therapists, behavioral analysts and occupational therapists.
- Access to electives, clubs and extracurricular activities that build skills and social connections.
- Philosophies on inclusion, restraint/seclusion policies, academic priorities and fostering independence.

Visiting programs can help gauge which environment aligns well to your child's needs at this point in their development and your family's priorities. Of course, ideal settings may evolve over time as skills and challenges change. Maintain an open and discerning mindset.

Embracing the Journey

Though aspects of navigating school pose challenges, maintaining loving perspective helps make the journey positive. Focus on celebrating each gain - a lesson learned, a friendship forged, a goal achieved. Your unwavering support reminds your child they have all they need to continue reaching their full potential. Their future is bright!

Chapter 13

Comprehensive Medical Care for Children with Autism

In addition to therapeutic interventions, medical oversight is crucial to address associated health issues, explore medication options when needed, and coordinate care across specialties. Finding knowledgeable providers experienced in addressing autism's complexities greatly benefits quality of life. An integrative approach draws from both mainstream and complementary medicine.

Coordinating Care Across Providers

Children with ASD often require multiple medical specialists like neurologists, psychiatrists, gastroenterologists, immunologists and sleep medicine doctors. To maximize progress:

- Choose a pediatrician you fully trust to serve as the "medical home" overseeing referrals and integrative care. They should have knowledge and experience in working with children with autism to understand the needs of complex kids.
- Share developmental history, prior testing and records across providers so all have a comprehensive picture to guide care. Maintain current med list.
- Accompany your child to appointments when possible to advocate, take notes, and provide parent observations. Serve as their voice.

- Request consult notes be shared between doctors so coordinated next step recommendations can be made vs disparate advice.

- Keep a binder with medical history, prescription/supplement lists, symptom trackers, therapy reports and provider contact info to bring to all visits.

- Inform all providers of medications, supplements, dietary interventions, and alternative remedies being used. Watch for potentially harmful interactions.

- Provide frequent feedback on how new medications or treatments are impacting symptoms, progress and any concerning side effects. Help steer optimal care.

Open communication between the care team allows fine tuning treatment plans to your child's evolving profile and needs. You play a pivotal role in this process.

Common Co-Occurring Conditions

Autism itself does not directly cause other disorders. However, higher rates of certain health conditions are reported, including:

- **Gastrointestinal issues** – Constipation, diarrhea, reflux, abdominal pain and food intolerances/allergies are frequently seen. Contributing factors may include immune dysfunction, low fiber diets, poor fluid intake, sensory issues, yeast overgrowth, and permeability of the intestinal lining. To relieve constipation, increase dietary fiber, fluids, probiotics and physical activity. Use osmotic laxatives as needed. Test for celiac disease and food allergies. Treat yeast overgrowth with anti-fungal agents and Saccharomyces boulardii probiotics. Heal intestinal lining with bone broths, glutamine, quercetin and zinc supplements. Massage and movement help motility.

- **Epilepsy/Seizures** – Up to a third of individuals have seizures at some point, more commonly those with cognitive impairment. Requires prompt neurological treatment.

- **Sleep dysregulation** – Difficulty falling or staying asleep. Frequent wakings, early rising, night terrors, and poor quality sleep occur. Sleep studies often helpful.

- **ADHD** – Problems with impulse control, hyperactivity and inattention frequently overlap with autism. May complicate learning.

- **Anxiety Disorders** – Excessive unease in social situations, fear of change, restricted interests centering on threats, and avoidance behaviors are common. Can be debilitating.

- **Depression** – Withdrawal, loss of interest in activities, low mood, and isolation may stem from social disconnect, bullying or purposelessness.

- **Genetic Disorders** – Fragile X, Down syndrome, tuberous sclerosis and other chromosomal abnormalities may co-occur in a minority of ASD cases.

Careful tracking of concerning behavioral and physical symptoms helps inform referrals to appropriate specialists for further evaluation and treatment. Multifaceted solutions are often needed.

Mainstream Medication Options

While not universally appropriate or effective, certain psychiatric medications may be prescribed judiciously to:

- Reduce severe tantrums, aggression, or self-injury – Atypical antipsychotics like risperidone, aripiprazole and olanzapine may curb dangerous behaviors when other interventions fail. Requires very close monitoring for side effects like weight gain, metabolic changes and lethargy.

- Treat anxiety disorders and repetitive behaviors –SSRI antidepressants like fluoxetine or fluvoxamine may ease anxiety. Low dose stimulants can be trials for obsessive compulsive symptoms.

- Improve focus and impulse control – Stimulants like methylphenidate or guanfacine may help ADHD-like symptoms. However, benefits must be closely weighed against potential adverse reactions. Long term safety is debated.

- Stabilize mood – Mood stabilizers, lithium and some anticonvulsants aim to stabilize mood swings and emotional regulation, but efficacy in ASD is questionable.

- Regulate brain chemistry – Natural supplements like omega-3 fatty acids, vitamin B6, magnesium, zinc, and melatonin help rebalance excitatory and inhibitory neurotransmission. Best discussed with doctor who knows physiology.

- Improve sleep – Melatonin, clonidine and antihistamines like diphenhydramine used short term can aid sleep onset. Behavioral modifications should also be implemented.

Medications should never be the sole treatment method. Benefits are often enhanced when paired carefully with educational, behavioral and sensory integration therapies catered to the individual. Track your child's responses and be very cautious with dosing.

Exploring Complementary and Alternative Medicine

While more research is still needed, parents may wish to ask their doctor about the following complementary approaches that aim to address physiological irregularities underlying autism behaviors:

- **Probiotics** – Can improve gastrointestinal health and immune function which are often dysfunctional in autism. Address possible yeast overgrowth.
- **Dietary Plans** – Gluten-free, dairy-free, anti-yeast, anti-inflammatory and food allergy elimination diets may help subset with gastrointestinal or autoimmune components. Should be nutritionally sound.
- **Digestive enzymes** – Improve digestion and absorption of nutrients if gut dysfunction. Can reduce abdominal discomfort.

- **Supplements** - Folinic acid, methyl-B12, curcumin, carnosine, vitamin D3 and magnesium boost metabolism, immunity and neurological processes. Use of alternative detox regimens like chelation requires thorough vetting for safety.

- **Mind-body practices** – Massage, acupuncture, animal therapy and music therapy help reduce stress levels and improve connections.

- Cannabidiol oil – Derived from cannabis, CBD oil may calm severe behavioral episodes and anxiety if medical cannabis is legal in your state and carefully dosed under doctor supervision. Research still very limited.

Discuss any complementary medicine approaches you are considering in depth with both your pediatrician and an integrative medicine doctor to determine if they are reasonable options for your child's challenges. Learn proper dosing. Key is targeting core physiological imbalances driving behaviors through safe means.

Exploring the Biomedical Model

The integrative biomedical approach views autism as multi-systemic, not simply behavioral, in nature. The goal is to assess and address underlying medical issues that potentially contribute to symptoms like oxidative stress, inflammation, immune dysregulation, mitochondrial dysfunction, methylation defects, gastrointestinal disease, microbiome disruption and toxins through specialized lab testing. Potential biomedical interventions may include:

- Nutrient therapies – Amino acids like l-carnosine, vitamins, minerals and antioxidants help repair pathways. Fatty acids improve cell membrane fluidity. Address deficiencies.

- Detoxification support – Oral glutathione, regular IV Vitamin C, and magnesium promote elimination of heavy metals like lead and mercury. Controversial chelation requires strict oversight.

- Gut healing diets – Remove inflammatory foods. Anti-fungal agents, healing broths, probiotics and enzymes restore intestinal lining health. Check for pathogenic overgrowth.

- Immunomodulation – Low dose immunotherapy, IVIG, plasmapheresis, and treatment of chronic infections rebalance the immune system to reduce inflammation.

- Hormone regulation – DHEA, oxytocin, secretin and melatonin supplements address relative deficiencies.

- Hyperbaric oxygen therapy – Increases oxygen delivery for improved mitochondrial function and tissue repair. Mixed evidence of effectiveness.

- Pharmaceuticals – LDN, activated folate, intranasal insulin, and melatonin aim to correct neurotransmitter imbalances and metabolic issues.

The goal is to identify and rectify the biological processes underlying autistic behaviors, not just mask symptoms. This functional approach is considered helpful by many parents, but remains controversial in mainstream medicine due to lack of large scale studies. Pursuing intense biomedical interventions warrants thorough vetting to ensure safety, efficacy and proper oversight.

By learning about all evidence-based options, parents can make informed choices in assembling an integrative medical team to optimize their child's health and future. Each person's physiology and needs are unique. Stay open and hopeful!

Chapter 14

Other Diagnosis (PANS/PANDAS, MITOCHONDRIA, CANDIDA)

Often children with autism are diagnosed with other conditions that are affecting their health. The three primary one that we have seen with our child are:

PANS/PANDAS

What is this?   PANDAS stands for Pediatric Autoimmune Neuropsychiatric Disorders Associated with Streptococcal Infections. PANS is Pediatric Acute-onset Neuropsychiatric Syndrome. They refer to a hypothesis that some neuropsychiatric conditions like OCD and autism may be triggered by autoimmune reactions originally caused by infections like strep throat. Here are some key points:

- The theory is that strep or other infections trigger antibodies and immune cells to mistakenly attack healthy cells, particularly in the brain. This leads to inflammation (swelling) and sudden onset of psychiatric symptoms.

- Hallmark symptoms include acute onset of obsessive-compulsive disorder (OCD), tics, autism-like behaviors, anxiety, emotional lability, and motor abnormalities.

- It is believed to occur most often in childhood as the blood-brain barrier may be more permeable earlier in development.

- Diagnosis involves assessing symptoms and history, combined with tests for infection-fighting antibodies and inflammation markers in the blood and spinal fluid.

- Treatment may involve antibiotics, anti-inflammatories, steroids, IVIG, plasmapheresis, and other immunosuppressants to reduce immune overreaction. Psychiatric medications can help manage symptoms.

- The PANDAS/PANS theory remains controversial as definitive evidence of an autoimmune cause is lacking. But research continues, as the disorders share many characteristics.

In summary, PANDAS/PANS are conditions theorized to be caused by brain inflammation in response to various infections, leading to sudden, troubling neuropsychiatric symptoms mainly affecting children. More research is still needed.

There is no definitive treatment for PANDAS/PANS since it remains a hypothesized condition without an established cause or cure. However, doctors may approach treatment in a few ways:

- Antibiotics or anti-viral medications if a current infectious trigger is suspected. This aims to stop further immune response.

- Anti-inflammatories and immunosuppressants like steroids or IVIG to calm systemic inflammation and overactive immune cells.

- Plasmapheresis or immunoglobulin replacement to remove antibodies/immune complexes from the blood.

- Psychiatric medications like SSRIs and antipsychotics to manage OCD, tics, and other behavioral symptoms.

- Cognitive behavioral therapy to help cope with obsessive thoughts and compulsive behaviors.

- Temporary academic accommodation, if symptoms interfere with school performance.

- Addressing any nutritional deficiencies that could contribute to a hyperactive immune response.

- Complementary approaches like acupuncture, massage, and meditation for anxiety.

- Monitoring for future symptom relapses that may require additional interventions.

However, these treatment approaches are not curative and have variable effectiveness. The goal is to manage symptoms until the presumed autoimmune flare subsides. High quality clinical studies are still needed to establish proven treatment protocols. Open communication with one's pediatrician is key when considering management options.

MITOCHONDRIA

What is this? Mitochondrial dysfunction refers to when the mitochondria in cells do not function properly. Here's an overview:

- Mitochondria are structures within cells that generate energy in the form of ATP through a process called cellular respiration.

- Mitochondrial dysfunction means this energy production process is impaired. Cells don't get enough usable energy.

- It can be caused by genetic mutations affecting mitochondrial proteins or environmental factors like toxins.

- Signs include muscle weakness, neurological problems, developmental delays, fatigue, heart/liver/kidney dysfunction, and more.

- Diagnosis involves blood tests for levels of lactate, pyruvate and other byproducts indicating cellular respiration disruption. Genetic testing may reveal mutations.

- Treatments aim to support and promote mitochondrial health through supplements like CoQ10, Carnitine, Creatine, and alpha-lipoic acid. Lifestyle changes like diet and exercise can help too.

- In severe cases, assisted reproductive techniques can help prevent transmission of mitochondrial DNA mutations during conception.

- Research continues into gene therapy and drugs to manipulate mitochondrial pathways and optimize their functioning.

In summary, mitochondrial dysfunction is when the mitochondria in cells fail to produce adequate energy. This can have system-wide effects, especially in organs and tissues with high energy demands. Supporting mitochondrial health is the main treatment approach.

CANDIDA

What is this? Candida is a type of yeast that normally lives in small amounts in places like the mouth, skin, gut, and vagina. When there is an overgrowth of candida it can cause an infection known as candidiasis. Here are some key facts about candida:

- It is a fungus, most commonly the species Candida albicans. Other species like C. glabrata can also cause infections.

- Candida commonly causes infections in moist areas of the body like the mouth (thrush), vagina (yeast infection), and skin folds. Invasive candidiasis can affect the blood, heart, brain, eyes, bones, etc.

- An overgrowth of candida in the gut can cause a condition called intestinal, or gut candidiasis. Symptoms may include bloating, cramping, diarrhea, and gas.

- Risk factors for candida overgrowth include antibiotic use, weakened immune system, diabetes, nutrient deficiency, high-sugar diet, and physiological stress.

- In healthy individuals, normal gut bacteria and an intact immune system keeps candida levels in check. Disruptions to these can trigger overgrowth.

- Candidiasis is usually diagnosed through physical examination, cultures, or stool tests to identify high candida levels. Blood tests can check for invasive infection.

- Treatments include antifungal medications, probiotics, dietary changes, and addressing underlying conditions that support candida growth.

So in summary, candida is a opportunistic yeast that normally inhabits the body in small amounts, but can proliferate and cause infection given the right conditions. Managing candida levels is part of maintaining overall health.

Common treatments for candida overgrowth are:

- Diet changes - Eliminating sugars, refined carbs, and alcohol can help starve candida. A low-carb and low-sugar diet is often recommended. Probiotic foods can promote healthy gut bacteria.

- Antifungal medications - Over-the-counter, prescription, or herbal antifungals may be used to kill excess candida. Common options include fluconazole, nystatin, or caprylic acid.

- Probiotics - Supplements of Lactobacillus, Bifidobacterium and Saccharomyces strains can help restore normal gut microbial balance.

- Natural antifungals - Oil of oregano, olive leaf extract, garlic, and grapefruit seed extract may have antifungal properties. However, potency and quality varies.

- Reducing gut disruptors - Limiting use of antibiotics, corticosteroids, birth control pills, and other medications that can trigger fungal overgrowth.

- Treating underlying conditions - Managing issues like poorly controlled diabetes or immune deficiencies that allow candida to flourish.

- Alternative therapies - Methods like acupuncture, hydrotherapy, and massage have limited evidence but are low-risk options some find beneficial.

As with any condition, it's important to consult a healthcare provider to correctly diagnose candida overgrowth and determine appropriate treatment.

Chapter 15

Self-Care and Support for Parents

Raising a child with autism is uniquely rewarding yet intensely demanding. Making time for your own needs is essential but often neglected. Prioritizing self-care, maintaining social connections, and seeking support sustains you in being the best parent you can be during this journey.

Focusing on Personal Wellbeing

With countless therapies, meetings and research occupying your schedule, caring for yourself often gets placed on the back burner. But setting aside time to recharge brings positive ripple effects for your whole family.

Eat nutritious meals, exercise, and get adequate sleep - Seems obvious but critical to maintaining physical and mental health. Don't neglect basic self-care.

Take brief respites - Even a few minutes of deep breathing, laughter yoga or looking at nature photography can provide mini "resets" in your day.

Do activities you enjoy - Read, garden, craft, attend a class - whatever hobbies energize you. You need fun in your life too.

Treat yourself kindly - Don't dwell on perceived mistakes or set unrealistic expectations. You're doing the best you can.

Give yourself credit - Celebrate your extraordinary strength, resilience and love. Pat yourself on the back often!

Seek counseling if needed - A professional can provide perspective on stresses and guide healthier coping strategies.

Your wellbeing directly impacts your child. Honor your needs so you can be fully present.

Staying Connected

Strong relationships are vital to withstand challenges. Though demanding schedules often strain social ties, carving out time together prevents isolation.

Schedule weekly date nights with your partner - Hire a sitter and take turns picking fun outings.

Share the load with your spouse - Ensure you both get breaks. Don't become solely responsible for therapies.

Go out with friends - Stay involved in hobbies and community. Don't let autism consume your identity.

Visit loved ones - Take trips to see extended family. Visits lift your spirits.

Respect differences - Not all loved ones handle autism the same way you do. Appreciate their support, even if imperfect.

Cherish progress - Reminisce together over memories and share hopes for the future. Focus on the positive.

By sustaining fulfilling relationships and laughter in your life, you gain strength for each day's journey.

Building Your Support Network

It truly takes a village. Connecting with others who understand firsthand helps combat isolation. Locate support through:

- Local autism organizations - Check for parent support groups, trainings and recreational events.
- Online communities – Connect with other parents on social media. But beware of fraudulent treatments or negative voices.
- Respite care – In-home sitters give short breaks. Some nonprofits provide free respite services for qualifying families.
- School events – Meet other parents at IEP meetings, therapies or extracurriculars. Exchange ideas.
- Support groups – Share experiences in-person or online. Therapist-led groups teach coping techniques.

- Sibshops – Designed for siblings to connect with peers who have autistic brothers or sisters.
- Your team – Discuss feelings honestly with your child's providers. Ask about counseling services.

Don't allow pride or shame to prevent reaching out. Other parents can empathize and uplift like no one else. You are not alone.

Managing Challenging Emotions

An emotional rollercoaster is to be expected. Give yourself grace as you work through often conflicting feelings:

Sadness – Allow yourself to grieve dreams or expectations that may not be realized. With time, these feelings tend to lessen.

Anxiety – Some worry is natural but can be countered with mindfulness practices. Take it one day at a time.

Anger – Vent frustration in healthy ways, not at your child. Channel energy into progress.

Guilt – Let go of "what ifs" and mistaken blame. You are a devoted parent.

Hope – Believe in your child. Their future is bright. Each tiny gain is a win.

Gratitude – When challenges mount, actively notice your child's gifts and strengths. Savor the positives.

With a trustworthy support circle and commitment to caring for your emotional health, you will find reserves of fortitude you never imagined. Your child's journey is made easier by your dedication and love.

Chapter 16

Envisioning the Possibilities: Planning Your Child's Future

Though managing day-to-day autism needs occupies much mental bandwidth, taking time to envision possibilities and make long-term preparations ensures your child's needs will continue being met at all stages of their journey. This chapter covers transitions to come, options for continued education, employment, independent living, legal considerations, and more to equip parents to secure their child's best future.

Preparing for Major Life Transitions

Moving into new schools, graduating, starting vocational programs, first jobs, independent or group living and other transitions require adaptations. Ease these by:

- Creating photo books, video tours and social stories to prepare your child by getting familiar with new settings and expectations in advance. Make multiple visits.
- Drafting templated documents summarizing your child's needs, challenges, preferences and most effective behavioral supports to share with new providers, employers and caregivers. Help them see your child as a unique individual.

- Determining what skills need proactive focus during the transition period to set them up for success in the new environment. Work on these life skills diligently.

- Requesting the IEP team formally assess and embed goals related to transition skills like using public transportation, money management, household chores and job-related behaviors into programming 2-3 years prior to leaving high school.

- Shifting more responsibility to your child for expressing their needs, interests and introducing themselves to new people as they're able. Build self-advocacy skills.

- Researching requirements, eligibility criteria and enrollment timelines for local adult disability agencies and vocational programs so you're prepared well in advance. Waiting lists are common.

- Identifying recreational programs, clubs, volunteering and peer mentors to help build your child's social community, interests and relationships in new phases of life. Prevent isolation.

- Celebrating expanded confidence and independence after each transition milestone! Recognize their hard work.

Post-Secondary Education Options

After high school, educational paths to build practical skills and credentials include:

College – With structured supports, college is feasible for some. Begin at community college, take a lighter course load or pursue a modified degree program. Disability resource offices provide accommodations. Look for autism social groups on campus. Consider having a peer roommate or mentor.

Career and technical education – Public vocational rehabilitation programs and nonprofits teach hands-on job skills like food service, horticulture, computer tech, auto mechanics, custodial work, woodworking, retail skills and more based on interests and aptitudes. develops expertise in transferable roles.

Travel training – Direct instruction to safely navigate public transportation for commuting to work sites, college or community activities. Crucial life skill for independence.

Job coaching and internships – Build resume writing, interviewing and workplace behavior skills through workshops and temporary internships allowing your child to sample different environments to determine best job match.

Post-secondary life skills programs – For those needing more significant supports, focus is on continuing functional academic, communication, self-care, vocational and community participation skills in small group settings.

Identifying meaningful ways for your child to utilize strengths and develop expertise creates connection and fulfillment.

Evaluating Adult Living Options

As adulthood nears, assess if independent or supported housing arrangements would be more feasible:

Independent living – Would a roommate be helpful for companionship or monitoring safety? Explore in-home skills trainers and respite services to provide periodic support.

Supervised apartments – Staff available on-site for reminders with tasks like meals, medication management, bills and transportation but more autonomy than group settings. Typically serve higher functioning individuals.

Group homes – Supportive communal living facilities ranging from a few residents up to 15 or more. More oversight and assistance is provided 24/7 for those needing moderate to significant daily living supports.

Adult foster care homes – Share a private family residence where the parents provide lodging, meals and individualized care. More personalized than larger group homes. Contracted pay.

Living at home with family – Being a lifelong primary caregiver requires honesty about if this is sustainable for your family's needs and realistic care plan with formal support services.

Visiting potential facilities, meeting housemates and asking about available amenities, staffing, activities, safety measures and oversight policies helps determine which option aligns best with your adult child's skills, challenges and personality after weighing positives and limitations of each. Some young adults try several arrangements as preferences evolve.

Securing Financial and Legal Resources

There are many avenues for financial and legal assistance including:

- Apply for Social Security Income (SSI), Medicaid waiver programs and state vocational rehabilitation funding if eligible. These provide monthly income and offset disability-related costs.

- Explore establishing a special needs trust which provides funds for your child's supplemental needs while allowing them to remain eligible for government disability programs. Can be funded by family or third parties.

- Evaluate choice of limited conservatorship or guardianship when your child turns 18. Which allows needed parental decision-making in areas like medical care and housing while preserving autonomy? Consult an attorney.

- Update your will and estate plan to ensure continuity of care instructions and financial support upon your passing. Set up an inheritance if desired and select trustees or guardians wisely.

- Create a detailed letter of intent for current and future caregivers relaying your wishes regarding ideal living situation, social activities, medical care, behavioral supports, and faith preferences.

By making legal and financial provisions, you gain peace of mind knowing comprehensive care according to your values can continue consistently throughout their adulthood.

Building a Supportive Community

A fulfilling life is not defined by independence in all areas, but rather experiencing meaning, purpose and belonging. Strategies to nurture community:

- Help them connect with peers through recreational clubs, Special Olympics, arts and music therapy groups, young adult ministries. Build lasting social relationships.

- Ensure they have creative outlets to express themselves like painting lessons, dance classes or journaling and share their gifts with others.

- Assign responsibilities matching their capabilities like household chores, volunteer work or part time employment that reinforces they have valued roles to play.

- Assist making and keeping longstanding connections with extended family members, mentors from school days and close family friends. Sustained relationships enrich lives.

- Explore integrative multi-generational housing communities that blend features of group homes, coworking and community life. These foster inclusive micro-societies.

- Use technology like social media, video calls and shared photos to help them stay connected when geographic proximity is a barrier.

With supportive networks, each individual can experience connection and purpose. Community is essential to wellbeing.

Exploring Fulfilling Daytime Activities

For higher functioning adults, provide coaching as they explore integrated or specialized job options that align with their interests and abilities or pursue post-secondary academics. Offer encouragement as they find their path.

Volunteer positions allow them to contribute, learn teamwork and gain dignity. Roles like stuffing envelopes, delivering meals, walking dogs at the shelter or gardening provide social outlets.

Adult day programs offer continued learning, recreation and friendship for those requiring more oversight and care. Arts, music and swimming activities foster joy.

Peer mentorships provide opportunities to share their skills assisting other autistic teens practice life skills like navigation or household tasks. Boosts confidence.

Identify any entrepreneurial interests with support turning into small home-based business ventures like baking, jewelry making or proofreading services. Creativity unleashed!

An array of meaningful options exist for your adult child to continue pursuing passions and cultivating purpose. Each person's right to define their own version of happiness and fulfilled life is sacred.

Embracing Family Life Transitions Mindfully

Watching your child whose diapers you once changed now independently commute to activities, cook their own meals and form mature relationships naturally elicits mixed emotions. It can be hard releasing control. Focus on gratitude for the privilege of being part of their journey while embracing this new phase:

- Respect their burgeoning adulthood while providing wisdom and stability. Offer guidance but increasingly empower their voice in decision-making.

- Balance being available while proactively encouraging as much autonomy as their capabilities allow. Let natural consequences do some teaching.

- Maintain family traditions and close bonds while acknowledging your shifting roles. You'll always be their parent, now with less hands-on responsibility.

- Pursue neglected hobbies, travel and personal growth. This fresh perspective actually benefits your ability to support them.

- Manage worries by focusing on capabilities. Each step of progress equips them for the journey ahead.

- Savor your evolving relationship, even when letting go feels difficult. Your guidance provides the roots for them to continue branching out.

The future remains bright for your child as their potential unfolds day by day.

Your devoted parents' heart forever guides them onward.

Conclusions

I hope this information has been helpful. I have tried to cover as much as possible. Things we were told and learned during our now almost 3 year journey, since our daughter was diagnosed.

If you are a parent reading this book, please have faith and please don't blame God for these troubles. He is there to help you through this. He has told has 365 times in the Bible to not fear, that is one for each day. When you pray for healing, just know God hears our prayers, but the answers may not be want we want to hear or in the timing that you would like. Just love your child. I don't know how to do it any other way. Just taking a day at a time, doing the best for that day and then moving to the next day and not looking in the past.

The key thing you need in this journey is patience. Patience with your child, patience with your spouse, patience with your doctor, patience with schoolteachers, patience with your therapists.

If you are a physician reading this, please learn as much as you can and support the families that need your help. Be open to things that they did not teach you in medical school. Be open to bio-medical therapies, homeopathy therapies and more. Go against the flow, searching for solutions to solve the problems of your patients. Do whatever takes to help your patient, that is the oath you took as a physician.

www.ingramcontent.com/pod-product-compliance
Lightning Source LLC
Chambersburg PA
CBHW070933260726
48661CB00003B/978